Hildebrand's Travel Guide

HONG KONG
MACAO

KARTO+GRAFIK VERLAGSGESELLSCHAFT MBH

Publisher
K+G, KARTO+GRAFIK Verlagsgesellschaft mbH
© All rights reserved by
K+G, KARTO+GRAFIK Verlagsgesellschaft mbH
Schönbergerweg 15–17
6000 Frankfurt/Main 90
First Edition 1989
Printed in West Germany
ISBN 3–88989–113–6

Distributed in the United Kingdom by
Harrap Columbus
19–23 Ludgate Hill,
London EC4M 7PD
Tel: (01) 248 6444

Distributed in the United States by
HUNTER Publishing Inc.,
300 Raritan Center Parkway,
Edison, New Jersey 08818
Tel: (201) 225 1900

Authors
Hong Kong: Dieter Jacobs, Franz-Joseph Krücker
Macao: Dieter Jacobs

Edited by
Bernadette Boyle

Photo Credits
J. Breyer, C. J. Eicke, J. H. Euler,
Ch. Henze, W. Keller/Mauritius,
U. Vogel, D. Weigel, K. Wolff

Illustrations
Eckart Müller, Peter Rank, Manfred Rup

Maps
K+G, KARTO+GRAFIK Verlagsgesellschaft mbH

Translation
Bernd C. Peyer

Lithography
Haußmann Repro, 6100 Darmstadt

Type Setting
LibroSatz, 6239 Kriftel

Printed by
Schwab Offset KG, 6452 Hainburg/Hess.

Hildebrand's Travel Guide

Impressions
Photographs
Travel Experiences and Reflections

Information
Land and People
Your Travel Destination from A to Z
Useful Information
Contents

Supplement: Travel Map

Captions

1. World-famous view of Hong Kong from Victoria Peak, with the mountains of the New Territories in the background, fronted by the Kowloon Peninsula, the natural harbour at centre and the Central District in the foreground.

2. View of Aberdeen's junk harbour. Despite new housing projects, some 20,000 people still live permanently on the water in about 3,000 junks.

3. More than just a tourist attraction: floating restaurants in Aberdeen's harbour.

4.–8. Hong Kong is a product of its harbour. Ships, shipbuilding and ferry-boats continue to play a major role here today. Approximately 70,000 people live permanently aboard their vessels.

9. Ricksha-driver in Hong Kong: a dying profession. For years now the government has refused to issue new permits. The remaining ricksha-drivers earn most of their income as "photo models" for tourists.

10.–12. Elderly and youthful Hong Kong: Hakka ladies in traditional costumes enjoying a pipe, a venerable peasant and a young «jade dealer» in typical squatting position.

13. Children at play in the streets of Hong Kong. Even the narrowest alleys must do.

14. Colourful decorations form part of every religious ceremony, be it a wedding or a funeral.

15.–17. The markets are the heartbeat of this commercial metropolis. A "good" Chinese housewife will shop at least once a day for the fresh groceries needed for the three meals she prepares daily.

18.–20. Contrasting scenes along the streets: from backyard workshops and tiny stores to regal showcases displaying precious jade and porcelain which tempt not only tourists.

21. One apartment per window; not unlike life in a beehive. An example of housing projects of the 1960's.

22. Hobby-room, laundry and pantry: in view of the crowded living conditions, the roof also fulfils a domestic function.

23. "Wild" housing developments such as these corrugated-iron huts erected by refugees will hardly stand up to a tropical storm. Slowly but surely they are making way for government-subsidized apartment buildings.

24. Crooked alleys and steep stairways – typical for the Chinese "Old Town" in the traditional residential area surrounding Man-Mo Temple.

25. Market in the narrow streets dissecting Hong Kong's rows of buildings. Most of the groceries have to be imported, primarily from the People's Republic of China.

26. Freshwater-fish and poultry farming in the rural areas of the New Territories are two major products of the otherwise territorially very limited agriculture. Only 7% of the land can be used for agricultural purposes.

27. Victoria Peak, at 554 m (1,818 ft) the highest point on the island, towers above Aberdeen, a seaport on the southern part of Hong Kong Island which was once a pirates' nest.

28. Pastoral scene in the New Territories. Even in technically advanced Hong Kong the farmers continue to use their traditional "tractor": the water buffalo.

29. View of Ocean Park, world's largest oceanarium, and the southern part of the island of Hong Kong.

30.–32. In the villages of the New Territories and on the offshore islands, the Chinese pursue their traditional religions.

33.–35. Buddhism and Taoism dominate religious thought in East Asia.

36.–37. The lives of Buddhists and Taoists are not regimented by churches. Religion is an individual's private affair; even the smallest niches suffice for a modest altar.

38. Numerous myths concerning Hong Kong's past are still circulating. These also serve as motifs for highly colourful "department store" art.

39. A bridge approximately three kilometres (1.8 miles) long connects Macao with the offshore island of Taipa.

40. View of Macao's Inner Harbour and the Ilha de Lapa belonging to the People's Republic of China. The border traverses the Pearl River estuary.

41. The historical cannon on Penha Hill is aimed directly at modern Macao's gold mine: the Hotel-Casino Lisboa.

42. Macao's landmark: the façade of the Basilica São Paulo.

43. Small garden of the Leal Senado.

44. Statue commemorating Ferreira do Amaral, the Portuguese founder of Macao.

45. Europe in Asia: this house in Macao could just as well be standing in some small Algarve seaport.

46. Mass-produced hats.

47. Antiques don't necessarily have to be antique.

48. Portuguese tiling with elements of Chinese style.

49. The lights never go out in Hong Kong: the city at twilight, as seen from Victoria Peak.

Approach Path over the Rooftops

The jumbo jet approaches in a wide arch over the South China Sea. Below us the water is a greenish-blue, sprinkled with freckle-like spots of brown and tiny white dots – a few of the 235 islands belonging to the territory of Hong Kong. Between them the junks of the fishermen from the crown colony or the mainland. To the right appears Hong Kong Island, dominated by Victoria Peak, with its 554 metres (1,818 feet) the highest point on the isle. Crowded around its crest, hardly visible in the mist, some of the luxury villas of the richest among the rich. Below them the breathtaking skyline of Victoria, banking and business centre of the crown colony. Hardly a square metre that is not occupied by skyscrapers outreaching each other.

Suddenly the scenery changes: highrisers to the left and right of us, almost at the same level as the windows and alarmingly close, and rooftops, just a few metres – or so it seems – below us. The aircraft continues to descend, touches ground and, just as abruptly, there is water all around us again – as if we were racing directly for the harbour basin.

Nevertheless, we are back safely on solid ground. The aircraft reduces its speed along the runway jutting out into the sea, turns and rolls towards the terminal of Kai Tak International Airport. "Welcome to Hong Kong", the voice on the loudspeaker comfortingly announces. Hong Kong's airport has one of the world's most difficult approaches and enjoys a rather notorious reputation among pilots. However, the international airlines only permit their most experienced and specially-trained pilots to take over the controls here.

The huge doors of the aircraft open. Now, at the end of April, a gust of hot and humid air takes our breath momentarily. It gets even hotter and more humid during the summer months, and the humidity remains even during the cooler winter.

Passport control is efficient and friendly, and the luggage, too, rolls in after a few minutes. Customs takes less than a minute and then we are in the midst of it – the greatest and most fascinating chaos in the world. All around us, people are bustling and rushing, pushing and pulling, shoving and squeezing. And yet things seem to happen in a composed and non-aggressive, almost disciplined, manner. The only stationary haven in this teeming mass seems to be the counter of the Hong Kong Tourist Association, where serene and friendly hostesses are happy to help out recent arrivals.

The way to the taxis is through the hall, and left of the exit. The queue here is longer than the one over on the right-hand ramp, where luxury hotel limousines pick up guests with confirmed reservations, but this does not cause it to break asunder. All arrivals calmly maintain their places; the British have exported proper "queuing" practices even to their remotest colonies.

If it were not for the luggage, at certain times of the day one would get about better on foot than by taxi. During rush hour the pace slows down to a crawl. The streets are as crowded as the rest of the city with its 5.5 million inhabitants. Wide, four-lane thoroughfares crisscross the city, but they can hardly contain what probably amounts to one hundred thousand cars on the road at one time.

So we simply lie back in the taxi and try to digest the impressions flooding in on us: the masses of people getting on or off buses, streaming out of underground stations, shopping centres and office buildings only to disappear into them once again. Hardly a spot within our range of vision that is not being torn down or built up, straightened or furrowed, hollowed out or elevated. Open spaces are rare indeed, especially here on the Kowloon Peninsula, where skyscrapers stand side by side and 200,000 people per square kilometre live in cramped quarters. (By way of contrast: the population density in England is approximately 354.5 per sq. km.)

The traffic is thinning out. Our taxi is able to move along at a good clip on the modern thoroughfare – towards Tsimshatsui East, the newer part of the city, which is surprisingly, and atypically, spacious. We recall

that a few years ago waves coming in from the harbour still struck the shore here; then earth was dumped in the water, the land reclaimed and soon a jungle of ugly, fallow land with occasional scaffolds emerged.

Today, huge shopping centres with thousands of stores stand here along with six super-modern, luxurious hotels separated from each other by green open spaces with playgrounds. Along the shore runs the harbour promenade, one of Hong Kong's newest attractions. As can be expected, the concrete construction has been built out over the ocean – the city has no land to spare. A few stray tourists are wandering about, photographing the view of Hong Kong Island, before which an old junk in full sail is bobbing across the harbour basin. At weekends, our driver informs us, this place is swarming with promenading Hong Kong Chinese, some of whom are even armed with fishing rods. What can one catch here in the harbour basin? Some kind of small fish apparently, which, when boiled together with vegetables, makes a fine soup.

Nathan Road seems to be the main artery of the Kowloon Peninsula. Here, buying and selling has become the essence and meaning of life. Gaudy signboards advertise watch and camera stores, jewellery shops, Indian or Chinese taylors, department stores, restaurants and cheap-jack shops, which together offer just about anything a tourist may desire. It is practically impossible to count the total number of stores. No wonder then that a large, international hotel chain has named its establishment on Nathan Road the "Golden Mile".

Our taxi stops in front of the hotel. A liveried doorman throws the doors open and a uniformed porter, who has already taken the luggage out of the boot, motions us towards the reception. Hong Kong's touristic rhythm confronts us in the spacious hall.

A group of Japanese storm the elevators, a flight crew checks out, a number of German tourists gather for the evening's "dinner-cruise" across the harbour, a couple of Americans wearing the inevitable Bermuda shorts and loaded down with bulging plastic shopping bags make themselves comfortable at the bar, an Australian tour guide searches frantically for two missing guests and businessmen carrying briefcases hurry between elevators and reception, from the entrance to the cafeteria.

The formalities are quickly taken care of and, following a friendly and personal welcome, we are sent on our way to the elevator and up to our room. Five minutes later the page closes the door behind him. We let ourselves sink into the chairs. Less than an hour ago we landed at Kai Tak and already we are overwhelmed with impressions, nearly exhausted by the hectic pace of this city. A cool drink and a little respite – and below us Hong Kong continues to pulsate.

(Jacobs)

Chinese City

One week on the Trans-Siberian Railway through the expanses of the Asian part of the Soviet Union and through Mongolia, followed by a three-week tour off the beaten track in the People's Republic of China – impressive, to be sure. And then Hong Kong. Truly a contrasting programme.

Today, the departure from the People's Republic proceeds as smoothly as one could possibly desire. Gone are the days when travellers had to get off the train at the border and carry their own luggage across the famous bridge by Lo Wu in order to board the Hong Kong commuter train. In Guangzhou (Canton) we climb on the direct train to Hong Kong. Air conditioning and a beverages service provide for a relaxed atmosphere during the three-hour trip. What will Hong Kong have in store for us after a four-week, thoroughly organized tour? Liberty, chaos, or both?

The train is a sort of world in between, symbolizing the separation and connection between the two facets of China on either side of the (yet) well-guarded border. The People's Republic had already taken leave of us in Guangzhou; passport control and customs formalities had not taken long. The customs officials in their new, green uniforms and red collar patches had only been concerned with currency declarations and the re-exportation of our camera equipment. A much more thorough inspection can be expected if the customs officials receive notice of a possible attempt to smuggle antiques. Their chain of information reaches all the way to Tibet.

Even the luxuries on board the train are atypical for the People's Republic. They are meant to demonstrate to the fellow countrymen in the capitalist metropolis that the comrades in charge of tourism and the railway system can also offer quality service. Or could it be that the Hong Kong Chinese have here, too, extended their long fingers into the vast domain, as in the case of the numerous recently-built hotels? As the train makes its way through Shenzhen, it becomes clear that this special economic zone in the People's Republic is, to a far greater extent than the railway, a symbol of the symbiosis between Communist Chinese efforts at economic development and Hong Kong Chinese capitalism.

Beyond Shenzhen, last city on the People's Republic's side, the scenery is briefly transformed back again to rice fields and orchards. But Hong Kong's hinterland is narrow indeed, and the concrete constructions designed to accommodate its ever-growing population are steadily advancing upon the border. Twenty to thirty storeys piled on top of one another, just seventy metres (230 feet) wide: more like walls than towers, standing close together like rows of dominoes. Unthinkable if one of them should fall. One can see at a glance that the apartments are cramped. The balconies are crowded with boxes, crates and even chicken coops, which in turn remind one of the People's Republic. Laundry seems to be hanging everywhere.

The train slows down and it becomes dark: we have arrived at the fully enclosed railway station. We make our way directly from the platform to the arrival's hall. The queue of voyagers moves quickly past Her Majesty's civil servants, whose royal blue uniforms and oriental features seem to embody some of the contradictions and multifariousness characterizing this city.

Our hotel is located on Hong Kong Island. Once again, organized transport in the hotel bus, the distribution of rooms and, finally, the whole day and Hong Kong itself are "at our disposal".

Outside again, among the milling crowd. But then, we are already used to that. At first, we are awed and somewhat dazed by the many palacial glass constructions. It seems that Hong Kong needs "overhauling" more frequently than other cities do. The buildings have to attain ever greater heights, because the available space is fast disappearing. Investments have to amortize in shorter periods, as no one knows what tomorrow or the day after will bring. The housing quarters began to crop up during the 1950's, when the steady stream of refugees threatened to inundate the city. Most of these buildings, especially those in the inner city, have already made room

for new generations of skyscrapers. The word "skyscrapers" can be taken literally here, because more than just the tops of the buildings vanish in a haze on rainy days.

Today, however, the sun smiles benignly from an azure sky. The best way to get around the northern coast of Hong Kong Island is with the old double-decker tram. It rolls along the tracks like some memento of bygone days, even though it only recently celebrated its 80th anniversary!... and didn't have a solid roof until 1923. But Hong Kong prefers a faster pace and ever since the subway made its appearance here, the none too nostalgic city planners want to get rid of the trams. And yet, as long as they continue to transport a half

million passengers per day, no one can really do without them.

From the front seat up on the top deck we watch the city clang by. At times we find ourselves leaning backwards in order to avoid crashing into an oncoming tram or some corner of a building. This spontaneous reaction persists in spite of what we know about the nature of rails! Once in the Central District, our first impression of an ever-expanding city is verified beyond all doubt. Here, no more than a few piled up bricks remain of the old, colonial Hong Kong.

But our actual destination is the true Hong Kong, the undying, Chinese Hong Kong. Beginning at Western Market, the street-gradient increases progressively – the Peak makes its presence felt. Wing Lok Street seems to be inundated with filled sacks. Store after store; lack of space causes them to spread out onto the pavement. And, as is apparently the case all over the world, at a certain period of development all manufacturers working in one field set up their businesses on a particular street. Golden days for consumers, because they could easily keep track of supply, quality and price. In Hong Kong, as everywhere, this is only possible today if one is searching for things old. Thus, Wing Lok Street is lined with chemists' and herbalists' shops. The dealers keep their goods in hundreds of glass jars; they weigh a few grammes for their customers with manual scales, empty the contents into small paper bags and, more than likely, add a few words of advice as they hand them over.

Finally, in the section behind Bonham, we again have the feeling of being in China. In fact, things here appear to be more "Chinese" – if there even is such a thing – than in the large cities of the People's Republic. Over there things proceed in a much too orderly, almost ordered, fashion. Here there is the street of the locksmiths; around the corner carpenters are busy sawing wood; two streets farther up is the turf of their specialized colleagues who still make traditional coffins out of a single log rather than nailing a few boards together. In the street that follows it is life that matters, because this is where the numerous vegetable markets are located. Here, too, people go shopping each day so that fresh vegetables, meat or fish be pleasing to the family's palate. Oftentimes the grocer will have a pocket calculator lying next to the cash register, but just to be on the safe side he may well add up the bill once again on the thousand-year-old abacus.

Wang Chai is in his mid-fifties and a shoemaker, just as his father was before him. It was from him that he inherited this tiny shop, hardly ten square metres in size. He sits in one corner on a low stool and is busy glueing and nailing before his improvised workbench. The sewing machine stands in the other corner. Pairs of shoes cover the walls, because Wang also makes new shoes whenever he has some time between repairs. And business is going quite well. "Fortunately I have a few old customers", he says, "and they would never go to one of those stores and buy shoes with plastic soles.

Unhealthy and too expensive they are; not much that can be repaired either. Bad for business." His shop smells of leather.

After a brief side-trip to the Man Mo Temple, tucked away in the middle of this bustling world, we finally arrive at our destination: Cat Street. Officially it doesn't even exist, because on city maps it is called Lascar Street. People here, however, see it differently. "Thieves' Market" they call the corner on Hollywood Road, and that may well be so. No one can really say where all of the "antiques" on offer came from. Some were brought in as valuables by refugees, while others were either smuggled across the border, obtained as heirlooms or specially prepared.

In East Asia people don't differentiate strictly between original and copies, as they tend to do in Europe. If the copy is good, it also commands its price. In some schools of art it was even considered worthy to copy the master's original as closely as possible – for centuries.

It is possible to find just about anything in the countless shops along Cat Street. There are books, vases, tea sets, jewellery, Buddha figurines, coins, seals, opium pipes, clothing, furniture, clocks, folding screens, aquarelles, ink drawings, bird cages and all sorts of junk.

The old trader is happy to see Europeans enter his shop, because they usually end up buying something. He is somewhat less elated, however, by the fact that he can't really bargain with them as it should be. Of course, all pieces are originals; the only problem is finding out just how each party defines said concept.

We rummage among the books, wander along the shelves filled with figurines and finally come across something that totally embodies the Chinese dichotomy, something that can no longer be found on the open market in the People's Republic and yet is lying about on some shelf in its capitalistic antipode: Mao's bust, made of shining white porcelain. The "Great Chairman" with the wart smiles complacently. Has he only managed to survive here? Is he heralding a new age? Or is he merely an antique? Original or a copy?

(Krücker)

Strolling along Temple Street

When night falls in Hong Kong, life begins. Temple Street changes into Kowloon's nighttime market, where, we are told, one can find anything that is a bargain. We halt at the entrance, consternated by the mass of people, the shoving and pushing amidst the narrow aisles flanked by lighted stands, doubting whether there is still room enough for us. But the new arrivals behind us and our own curiosity urge us forward; we let ourselves be pushed and pulled along, look around and become a part of the Chinese retail business scene.

Directly to the left is a stand selling cheap records and cassette tapes. Michael Jackson's latest hits blare from loudspeakers along with those by Taiwanese pop singer Deng Lijun and newly-recorded interpretations of Springtime in South China on the erhu, the ancient Chinese two-stringed instrument.

A textiles dealer to the right grabs my arm and pulls me over to his stand. His merchandise is cheap jeans – the artsy trademark of a renowned company is displayed on the back. «Only thirty dollars», he says and as I hesitate he lowers the price to 25 HK-Dollars, undoubtedly much less than what the trademark jeans retail for. But then, at that price even an imitation seems like a good deal.

Nevertheless, the dealer has mis-interpreted my hesitation: after all, where should I try them on? Right here in the middle of the street? I signal "No, thanks" and want to go on, but by then the next dealer has me in his grip. The cheapest T-shirts around, he assures me. Apparently he is particularly fond of one he insists on showing me after finding out where I come from. He digs around in a carton and finally finds it on the bottom. Proudly he holds it up to me. It is white and bears a huge emblematic eagle over the words: German Soccer League. Now I am

grateful for the milling crowd into which I can quietly disappear.

Not an inch of room is left unused here as stand follows stand. Some dealers loudly present their wares, others sit by indifferently as we look over what they have to offer. There are lighters, ballpoint pens, watches and pocket calculators lying about everywhere – some supposedly made by Cartier, Dunhill, Dupont, Rolex or Seiko, all for less than one hundred HK-Dollars. Nearly perfect imitations, as long as one only looks at them superficially. But everyone shopping here knows they are imitations and thus not a single customer ever feels cheated.

In between all this there are always cooking stands where one can sit down to a bowl of rice with boiled fish and vegetables or fried pork or poultry with noodles. The cooks don't mind at all if foreign visitors peek inside pots and woks. It facilitates communication and choice, so that every foreigner gets a chance to try a light evening snack. Afterwards one can go over to the next stand and help the digestion along with a large cup of bitter-tasting, green herbal tea.

This lively commercial activity on Temple Street goes on until well past midnight, almost into the morning hours. A similar evening market takes place on the Hong Kong side, on the parking lot over by where the ferries to Macao and the islands dock. It bears the distinctive and famous name of "Poor Man's Nightclub".

(Jacobs)

The Menu

Willie Mark is Hong Kong's king of gourmets. Whether it be international European cooking, "nouvelle cuisine" or one of the various Chinese or other Asian culinary arts – his word is law. There is hardly a hotelier, restaurant-owner or chef around who does not ask for Willie Mark's advice or opinion if he is about to open some restaurant or introduce a new culinary creation. The gastronome, journalist, hotel- and restaurant-advisor, advertizing expert and hobby-cook reflects his fifty years of good living: he is all-round round.

We are sharing a table at "Sun Tung Lok Shark's Fin", a restaurant in Kowloon's super-modern shopping centre, "Harbour City", and enjoying horse-neck clams (flown in daily from arctic waters), oysters (naturally), fresh shark's fin soup, garupa (a very tasty fish), prawns, noodles, steamed vegetables and fried rice, to the accompaniment of whisky and tea. Meanwhile, Willie Mark explains the philosophy behind Chinese cooking to me: "It's very simple – everything has to be fresh; spices are used sparingly, neither too hot nor too rich, so that the taste of meat, fish, poultry or vegetables is not adulterated. Everything is chopped down to bite-size and then steamed, cooked or fried for a much shorter period of time than is common in Europe."

This also explains the popularity of the produce markets in the metropolis. Willie Mark: "The average Chinese housewife goes to the market at least once a day in order to buy fresh vegetables, meat, fish, fruit and salad. Canned or frozen foods are not served at our tables. In the rural areas of the New Territories it is even customary to go to the market twice daily: in the mornings for what is needed for lunch and in the afternoon for dinner."

This is why Chinese food is so wholesome; the tea served with it is also supposed to be good for the digestion. At least foreigners will come to know the advantages of eating slowly when they try to eat with chopsticks. They will have no trouble learning the technique if they hold the lower chopstick between the inside of the thumb and the palm of the hand and let it rest on the ring finger. The upper chopstick is movable; it rests along the index finger much like a dart and is held by thumb, index and middle finger. A Chinese waiter or waitress will show you how to use them and be pleased by your efforts.

Before going into more detail, however, Willie Mark clears up a few misconceptions that newly-arrived Western visitors tend to have concerning "Chinese food": chop suey probably originated in Indonesia, but even there it is considered a leftover rather than a traditional dish; sweet-and-sour pork was created especially for foreigners, who, it was thought, liked to eat sweet food. And he goes

on to explain something else that is basic: "A meal has to tempt all your senses. That is why it has to look good as well as smell and taste good. It has to be prepared with human and natural conditions in mind. No one would eat snake or dog meat in the summer." This kind of meat warms one from the inside and is thus a typical winter meal. Which brought us to the subject of Cantonese specialties. "Supposedly the Cantonese eat anything that moves, but the preparation of dog, for instance, is prohibited and thus will only occur in secret. And there is little chance that a foreigner will be served delicacies like monkey brains or bear paws. You may rest assured of that."

And so Willie Mark describes the most important Chinese culinary traditions:

– **Cantonese** cooking is the traditional cuisine in Hong Kong. Besides fish and seafood, it is made up of lightly boiled vegetables and poultry, including pigeon, quail and, above all, chicken. Practically all dishes are cooked very quickly in a little water and oil in a wok. The Cantonese steam vegetables and fish so that the natural flavour is preserved. Sauces are often composed of contrasting ingredients such as vinegar and sugar or ginger and onions. Food is seasoned well but not excessively.

– **Fujian** cooking favours pork, duck and duck eggs, as well as fish and seafood. Various ingredients are combined in the preparation of omelettes and pancakes. Pork fat is frequently used in cooking, which can make a few dishes rather greasy. Soups are also quite popular. Rice cakes and tarts from Fujian are now commonly found all over Southeast Asia, as a great many immigrants originated from this province.

– **Shanghai** cooking is also dominated by fish and seafood. A meal of-

49

Dim Sum

Whoever told me that one can eat in peace and quiet in a Hong Kong restaurant has never been to the "Luk Yu Tea House" on Stanley Street, in Hong Kong's Central District. People are constantly coming and going, chairs are moved around and there is lively conversation followed by laughter coming from every table. Next to me a baby whines while its grandmother calls the waitress from the other end of the establishment in order to pay her bill.

But then, Willie Mark, Hong Kong's king of gourmets, didn't promise me peace and quiet when he insisted that I try some *dim sum* if I really wanted to say – not to mention write – something about Cantonese cooking.

Translated verbatim, *dim sum* means "touch the heart" and that is indeed what these delicate titbits will do. The Cantonese prefer partaking at lunch, which simply means that *dim sum* is not available for dinner and that *dim sum* restaurants are quite crowded at noon. And correspondingly loud. Nevertheless, I immediately fell for *dim sum:* for *har gau* (stewed prawn dumplings), *shiu mai* (stewed ground pork with prawn dumplings), *pai gwat* (braised spareribs with red pepper sauce), *ho yip fan* (lotus leaves filled with fried rice), *ham shiu kok* (pork, prawns and vegetables in rice dough) and *tsun guen* (egg rolls filled with ground pork, chicken, mushrooms, bamboo-shoots and beans). A sweet dessert completes the meal: *ng lau jar wan tun* (fried dumpling with sauce), *daan sarn* (sticky-sweet cake with chopped almonds) or *hung dow sa* (sweet soup made from red bean paste).

The way to order is absolutely simple and therefore that much more enticing. Waitresses and waiters come by the tables carrying trays or pushing carts and call out what they have to offer. For foreigners they will lift the lids to reveal the dishes beneath. You just nod and the titbit in question will be placed before you on a plate or in a small bamboo basket. Now all you have to do is go to it with your chopsticks. Connoisseurs never say thank you or "um goi"; instead, they tap the table twice with the tips of their fingers, in accordance with an ancient Chinese tradition.

The waitresses are very generous with tea servings. I have hardly taken a sip from my cup and already it is being refilled. Settling accounts is just as uncomplicated: the empty plates and baskets remain on the table and all the waitresses or waiters have to do is count them and multiply the sum by two to three HK-Dollars. For a mere 20 HK-Dollars you can eat your fill.

Dim sum is generally served from early morning until late afternoon. At the "Luk Yu Tea House", for instance, from 7:30 am to 5:30 pm. The Hong Kong Tourist Association has a *dim sum*-brochure available, which contains a description of the various dishes.   *(Jacobs)* ten begins with a platter of cold hors d'œuvres. This is followed by dishes that have been either deep-fried or coated in batter and fried. Highly recommendable is the spicy-sour soup which, of course, is eaten at the end of a meal to help digestion.

– **Szechwan** cooking offers the greatest variety, and is also the hottest. This southern Chinese province is considered to be China's foremost agricultural area. The Chinese call it "Kingdom of Plants and Animals" and a few of these obviously end up in the wok. The spices used in the southwest are particularly hot. Szechwan pepper, chilli, garlic, ginger, cinnamon and coriander enrich the flavour of pork, duck and chicken while making the person enjoying the meal break out in a sweat. But vegetables are also an essential ingredient, as is rice. After all, the latter is harvested three times a year in Szechwan.

– **Peking** cuisine, as a representative of the north, ist entirely different. Actually it should be referred to as Mongolian cooking, because over the centuries it adopted many dishes from the far north, especially from the Manchus and Mongolians. Wheat instead of rice is cultivated in this region and as a consequence bread and noodles are part of the staple diet. The best-known dish, of course, is the Mongolian firepot, a soup served simmering over burning charcoal and supplemented with thin slices of meat an vegetables. Here, too, chopsticks should be used to fish the latter out of the broth, but those beginners who are particularly

hungry may ask for a small sieve. The firepot is a typical winter meal.

But then, what would Peking cooking be without Peking duck? A particular species of duck ist butchered after about 65 days and then slowly grilled. In the process, the skin is basted again and again with a syrupy sauce until it becomes brown and crispy. The chef will then show the guests the entire bird, expecting approbation. After this it is chopped up into small, bite-sized pieces which are rolled inside thin flour cakes with soya bean paste, green onions and cucumbers and eaten with the fingers. A powerful brandy will ease digestion. Finally, a soup will be served that has been prepared in the meantime from the bones of the duck, vegetables and herbs.

Cantonese cooking may be dominant in Hong Kong, but Chinese immigrants from all parts of the country have brought their culinary traditions with them to their new domicile. Indeed, opening up a restaurant is one of the favourite activities of Chinese abroad. Thus all regional Chinese cuisines are represented in Hong Kong, along with those from many other areas in Asia. One can find Korean, Japanese, Vietnamese, Philippine, Indonesian, Malaysian, Thai, Indian and even Burmese cooking here. European cuisine (including Italian, French, Greek and that of other Balkan countries) is also represented. Steak houses and hamburger chains have also made their appearance recently, but one can easily avoid them. Generally, those who hesitate to try Asian food in Asia will pay the penalty of higher prices.

The larger hotels usually have several restaurants, one of which will be serving Western food while the others specialize in Asian dishes. The quality of the food is generally very good, although the chefs have often adapted themselves to Western tastes.

Visitors should not fail to take advantage of a very special treat available during the summer months (June to October): a fish and seafood dinner on Causeway Bay's sampan harbour. One hires one of the small sampans, which are modelled after the larger junks, and allows oneself to be skippered around the harbour.

The meals are served on other sampans lying out in the harbour: crabs, prawns, mussels, oysters and fish are offered, as well as meat, vegetables and beverages. Female skippers prepare the meals on board with portable gas stoves. A delicious dinner that you will certainly never forget.

Undoubtedly better known are the "floating restaurants" along Aberdeen's junk harbour. These are not actually floating, as they are anchored to the bottom by concrete pillars. They do not only serve as tourist attractions, but also as a place where locals like to hold banquets. Cognoscenti, however, prefer going there during lunch hours when traditional *dim sum* is served.

(Jacobs)

The Wine List

There is nothing that can't be had in Hong Kong: a principle which also applies to beverages. Be it wine from the vineyards of France, Germany, Italy, Spain, California or Australia; beer from Munich, Dortmund or Scandinavia; or high-proof liquor from France, Scotland, Ireland, England, Kentucky or northern Germany – all of it is available and sometimes for less than it costs in the country of origin, thousands of miles away. The secret behind all this is taxation, which exists in Hong Kong but tends to be quite low.

In Hong Kong itself a beer is brewed under licence and sold under

the well-known brand name of "San Miguel". From the People's Republic comes the tasty "Qingdao" beer, a remnant of Germany's colonial past in northern China.

Chinese wines are not to be compared with European vintages. They are very sweet, much like liqueurs, and only to be consumed in small quantities. High-proof destillates are prepared from rice, grain, herbs or flowers.

"Siu Hing", also referred to as "yellow wine", is relatively mild and is made from rice. Its taste is quite similar to a mildly dry sherry and, served warm, it complements all varieties of Chinese cooking.

"Go Leung" and "Mao Tai" are the better known of the strong Chinese spirits. Distilled from grain, they can be up to 70% proof and are therefore recommendable as a digestif following a hearty meal, especially Peking duck.

"Ng Ka Pay", a sweet liqueur made from herbs and resembling Campari in taste, makes a good apéritif. Many Chinese laud its medicinal properties and recommend it as a remedy against rheumatism.

Aside from the above, there are still a number of wines and spirits that even the Chinese consider to be exotic, such as the one made from snake essence or the brand with a dead lizard floating in the bottle. It is said that these particular spirits are good for the circulation and eyesight.

However, it is Cognac rather than local spirits that the Cantonese like to consume on festive occasions. The statistics show that Hong Kong has the highest per capita consumption of Cognac in the entire world.

The ideal digestif, tea, should be part of every meal. In many restaurants tea will automatically be served with all dishes. If you do ever have to pay extra for it, it will be a matter of only a few pennies.

The three types of tea most commonly available are: green, unfermented tea; the black "Bo Lay", a fermented tea also referred to as "red tea"; and "Oolong", a half fermented tea.

Every region cultivates its own particular kind of tea; this is especially true of the southern and eastern part of China. The taste will depend upon the kind of tea planted, properties of the soil, and climate. As is the case with wine, the age can make a big difference. The youngest and, therefore, smallest leaves provide the best quality.

The Chinese prefer to drink their tea unadulterated. Requests for milk, lemon or sugar may very well meet with the disapproval of waiters, as these detract from the tea's special aroma.

On the other hand, flavoured teas are also quite popular with some: jasmine, chrysanthemum, rose leaves or narcissus.

Listed below are the names of a few of the more popular flavoured teas you might try out during your visit to Hong Kong: "Heung Pien", or jasmine tea; "Tit Kwun Yum" ("Iron Goddess of Mercy"); "Loong Ching" ("Dragon Well"); "Shui Hsien" ("Water Lily"); and "Bo Lay", named after a city in China.

By the way, Hong Kong has its own tea plantation on the island of Lantau. A tour can be arranged through the Hong Kong Tourist Association.

(Jacobs)

53

A Modern Family

"My sister's husband is also a *gwailo*," Esther says as we are introduced. *Gwailo* refers to us all, the non-Chinese, or "foreign devils" and barbarians. Esther and her husband Francis consider themselves quite definitely to be Han, or descendants of the first Chinese dynasty, that foremost civilization and culture.

Both Esther and Francis were baptized in their youth, but this is taken with a grain of salt around here. Even practising Christians in Hong Kong tend to follow a practical mixture of Christian teachings and traditional Chinese customs and rites. Thus Esther tells me how she went to a soothsayer prior to consenting to her marriage in order to ask the gods' favour. And Francis recounts how his father, also a Christian, contracted a *fung-shui* specialist, or earth-soothsayer, when they managed to find their small apartment surprisingly fast, so that he could make sure that the house was not standing on the head, comb or tail of a dragon.

Esther and Francis, both in their mid-twenties, are quite happy with their small apartment, which hardly measures 40 square metres (48 square yards) and is located near Happy Valley in Hong Kong. From the living room they can even catch a glimpse of the harbour and the lights of Tsimshatsui on the Kowloon side, in between the many towering apartment-houses fronting the window. The apartment, which swallows about 25% of their income, certainly wasn't easy to obtain, and their efforts would undoubtedly have been futile without the good connections of Esther's father. Since Esther is an executive secretary at a major insurance company and Francis a judicial officer, their collective income, and the fact that they have no children, disqualifies them from the subsidized housing projects of the city. Sure, that would have been much less expensive, but also that much more crowded. Francis tells of a colleague who lives in such an apartment near Shatin in the New Territories together with his wife and four children: they share some 20 square metres (24 square yards), that's about half the size of Esther's and Francis' apartment.

Household chores are divided between Esther and Francis democratically: whoever arrives home first from the office takes care of the apartment and prepares dinner. Both studied in the US, where they also met. Therefore they no longer believe in the old tradition whereby a woman is supposed to stand behind her husband. "With our parents", says Francis, "things are still that way. Our mothers' duties are restricted to the kitchen, household and family."

Children? "Yes, as soon as we can afford them", Esther explains. Presently about 80% of their combined income is spent on groceries and rent, 5% goes for transportation (they don't own a car), 5% is used up for services rendered and another 5% is expended on clothing and footwear. The remainder is either saved or invested; at times a little more, at times a little less. But they'll certainly have no more than two children.

Esther has four siblings and Francis three, but they only want as many children as they can afford to provide with an adequate education.

Education traditionally ranks high in importance in Chinese society. Of course they would rather have their future children study at one of the two universities in Hong Kong. The number of students that can be accepted, however, is limited and will continue to be so. Thus they already reckon with the possibility of having to send their children to study in the US and that will be expensive indeed!

(Jacobs)

Life on a Junk

Late afternoon of the next day I'm in Aberdeen with Esther and Francis. They had said previously that they wanted to show me the residence of the Wuh family. The couple, who are in their early thirties, live and work together with their six children and grandparents on board a seagoing junk. The two youngest members of the family, a boy and a girl, have a line tied around them so they won't fall off the deck while playing. "This has not always been so and still cannot be taken entirely for granted today", Esther comments. "Oftentimes only the boys are secured by a line while the girls are allowed to crawl about freely. If one of the latter should fall into the water it would not be so tragic – you see, according to Chinese tradition the females occupy a much lower position than the males."

Within the Wuh family, the role of the sexes is patterned along traditional lines: while Mr. Wuh and the grandfather join us in the cabin (which serves as both living-room and sleeping quarters) and offer their European guests the best of French Cognacs as an aperitif, Mrs. Wuh and the grandmother are preparing the food. Fish and seafood, we are told.

Modern-minded Esther feels somewhat uncomfortable in the all-male company. She decides to join the women and help them with the cooking being done on gas stoves. "Yes", says Mr. Wuh, "our women's first and foremost duties are in the kitchen and taking care of children. But out on the open sea, when we are fishing, they have to lend a hand just like the men."

Although the junk is much more spacious inside than it appeared from the outside, it is still way too small for ten people. The Wuhs would have preferred having fewer children, but they are dependent on the younger generation: "They are irreplaceable

as cheap labour and social security."
Grandfather Wuh smiles and nods in
approval – he doesn't understand a
word of English.

Beds are unknown on the Wuh's
junk. Woven straw mats are rolled
out when it is time to sleep. What
about the lavatories? All smiles, Mr.
Wuh points to the stern, to where it
juts out beyond the hull. I climb the
steep staircase, raise the lid and stare
directly at the dirty-brown waters of
Aberdeen's harbour.

"Don't be fooled", Francis says later
on in the evening as we are back on
land, "the Wuhs are not poor people.
A junk like that is worth a six-digit
sum." In Hong Kong, by the way,
some 70,000 people still live permanently on junks or smaller sampans.

All that remains to be said is that
the seafood served by the Wuhs in
Aberdeen tasted better than anything
I have ever eaten at the best seafood
restaurants around the world.

(Jacobs)

In the Beehive

Like every other morning, Mr. Ma clambers down the steep concrete stairs of his block of flats. In his right hand he carries a case with handles, made of simple black plastic: "Made in Hong Kong." At a leisurely pace he joins the already lively traffic on the streets. Most of the people about at this hour have the same destination: the underground. As part of the teeming throng, Mr. Ma disappears beneath the earth.

Like every other morning, the modern coaches are overcrowded. Mr. Ma leans against a partition, pulls a newspaper out of his pocket and tries to read. But the tiny letters covering the four-page paper dance before his eyes. Besides, he didn't sleep well again last night; his father's coughing fits have kept him awake for days.

Like every other morning, the ride on the underground takes almost a quarter of an hour, then Mr. Ma gets off and walks for another fifteen minutes. Finally, he disappears into an alley between the concrete towers of Tsimshatsui, walks through a door and then up three flights of stairs. He has arrived at "his" factory. Mr. Ma works as book-keeper for Mr. Fong, owner of twelve sewing machines, and is also responsible for all other paperwork that needs to be taken care of in Mr. Fong's enterprise. Mr. Ma is 53 and has been working for Mr. Fong for five years.

Like every other morning, Mr. Ma takes his teacup from the cupboard, rinses it out in the small washbasin next door, adds a few tea leaves and fills it with boiling water. Now the day can begin. He sits down on an old chair in front of a table covered with papers and begins to read anew the letter sent by the textile merchant. The abrupt rise in the prices demanded by the merchant angers him. Sewing machines rattle away in the background; the early shift has already been working for two hours. Everyone, including Mr. Ma, sits in the same room, which also functions as packing and storage space, Four women and eight men do piecework here, sewing together shirts after a set pattern.

A second shift takes over after they have done their eight and a half hours. Mr. Fong urges them to do a little overtime because he has been fortunate again. Twenty thousand shirts have been sold to a German chain establishment; only the dateline must be met. But Mr. Ma is busy calculating on his abacus. If only he could concentrate!

As always at noon, Mr. Ma descends the stairs, turns two corners and enters a small Cantonese restaurant. The waiters all know him and greet him accordingly. Mr. Ma, too, seems to liven up somewhat here. He orders noodle soup and takes a few sips of hot tea, which the waiter has placed on the table unasked. It is hot outside, but tea is still the most effective refreshment. Mr. Ma doesn't think very highly of this "coke" thing the young people like to drink. At lunch he meets up with acquaintances who also work closeby and they exchange a few words: the weather, health, horse races. On the way back to work, Mr. Ma weaves through the crowd on the pavement; traffic on the street is congested again. He stops in front of a shop window, lights a cigarette and thinks about his next acquisition: the whole family has been saving for a year to purchase a colour TV.

Like every other afternoon, following eight hours of work, Mr. Ma sets out to do some errands for his wife. His youngest child, who still attends school, needs a new notebook. And he also wants a pocket calculator. Mr. Ma buys the evening paper and stops for a moment to scan the headlines. Then he proceeds to the underground station.

At home, he dabs his face with water in the communal washroom, removes his shirt, rolls up his trouser-legs and seats himself on a stool in the hallway. In the meantime his wife is preparing dinner for the eight-member family. Along with Mr. Ma and his wife, four of their five children and Mr. Ma's parents share a 22-square-metre room – not even three square metres per person. One closet, three beds, three cots, a folding table, a bench and four stools comprise the furniture. And, of course, there's the television, which has obviously been on for hours. The youngest child is doing his homework on the folding table while mother slices vegetables. Cooking is done in a communal kitchen for 14 families. The neighbour's television is blaring out another programme and Mr. Ting on the other side is listening to his Peking operas again. He can really get on one's nerves. Mr. Ma lights up another cigarette and reads the paper. But just as he is beginning to relax, trouble arises again. His 16-year-old daughter doesn't feel like doing her washing after a whole day's work at the office. But her mother calls out from within that she can't manage to do it and that it is too strenuous for grandmother. So Mr. Ma hands his daughter a bucket and sends her out to the washroom.

Like every other evening, Mr. Ma sits with his family at the dinner table. Today there are two kinds of vegetables, a little bit of fish and a large pot full of rice. Everyone helps himself to the contents of the pots with his own chopsticks and transfers them to a bowl. The television is still on and thus there is very little conversation. It is the youngest's turn to do the dishes. He collects the dishes in a plastic bucket and makes his way to the washroom.

The Ma family pays 120 Hong Kong Dollars for their apartment, which is relatively little. The family's income is so low that it was able to obtain these subsidized quarters as many as 12 years ago. Conditions are very cramped and there are cartons piled up all over the place, even on the balcony. "Peace and quiet" are unknown to Mr. Ma and his family as well as every one else living on this block.

Like every other evening, all of the furniture has to be cleared away so that each member of the family can retire to bed. The second oldest son sleeps on the bench; the youngest on a mattress placed on the floor. Windows and the door to the hallway remain open; only the screen door is shut. And still the room remains sultry. Sometimes, in the evenings, a little breeze picks up.

(Krücker)

Of Noble Houses and Tai-pans

"Hong Kong will work its magic on you – or evil, depending how you see it. For business it's the most exciting place on earth and soon you'll feel you're at the centre of the earth. It's wild and exciting for a man; my God, it's marvelous for a man but for us it's awful and every woman, every wife, hates Hong Kong with a passion, however much they pretend otherwise... We're all threatened here... We women fight a losing battle..." This is how, in Clavell's *Noble House,* the sister of the tai-pan, the omnipotent boss of the largest trading house in Hong Kong, describes her situation and the city.

And she discloses a few more facts concerning Hong Kong to the newly-arrived American business partner: "Everyone here's pretty vengeful... one reason's because we're such a closely knit society, very interrelated, and everyone knows everyone else – and almost all their secrets. Another's because hatreds here go back generations and have been nurtured for generations. When you hate you hate with all your heart. Another's because this is a piratical society with

very few curbs, so you can get away with all sorts of vengeances. Oh yes. Another's because here the stakes are high – if you make a pile of gold you can keep it legally even if it's made outside the law. Hong Kong's a place of transit – no one ever comes here to stay, even Chinese, just to make money and leave. It's the most different place on earth... Another reason's that we live on the edge of catastrophe all the time: fire, flood, plague, landslide, riots. Half our population is Communist, half Nationalist, and they hate each other in a way no European can ever understand. And China – China can swallow us any moment. So you live for today and to hell with everything, grab what you can because tomorrow, who knows? Don't get in the way! People are rougher here because everything really is precarious, and nothing lasts in Hong Kong." – "Except the Peak... and the Chinese", interjects Penelope (the wife of the tai-pan).

James Clavell, himself an Australian-born globetrotter, uses this backdrop to present a powerful image of emotions and passions in this contra-dictory, extreme and challenging city. His invented protagonists, who are based in part on real figures, approach all aspects of their lives with veritable passion: the horse races, big business, espionage, food, love. Clavell's *Noble House* is set in the Hong Kong of 1963, during the turbulent days following the split between Moscow and Peking, before the Cultural Revolution and American participation in the War of Vietnam, when Hong Kong faced a serious economic situation. It is a story dealing with the economic power struggle and espionage between Washington, London, Peking and Moscow. The plot does have its historical parallels because scandals involving corruption and espionage did indeed shock Hong Kong's police force at the time. And the struggle between the two big men from the "houses" of Struan and Gornt goes on.

This struggle becomes clearer if one reads Clavell's other, and better, novel, *Tai-Pan.* It deals with Hong Kong's founding years, around 1841, and describes the struggles between British and American opium dealers and the Chinese *hong,* the imperially-sanctioned trading houses in Canton, as well as the British government and its local representatives, the soldiers and administrators. The main plot of Clavell's novel, however, is the legendary conflict between the two most powerful merchants, Dirk Struan and Tyler Brock; it is a conflict which centres around whose trading house ranks foremost and may thus be rightly called "noble house". Bribes,

intrigues, betrayal and bloody frays mark the conflict. Fate, or *joss,* intervenes again and again; and love, of course, plays a role. Obviously the characters in the novel are not authentic. Nevertheless, this is probably how they really were, those seasoned sea wolves of the Indian and Pacific Oceans who finally brought their hardened regiments on land – in Hong Kong. The actions and mentality of the Chinese are also described. In the long run – and this is also true historically – the Chinese always keep the upper hand, even then when the "barbarians" think themselves ahead and in control of Hong Kong. Dirk Struan, the tai-pan, is only able to win because he learns and partially adopts Chinese ways. Even his seal represents the real Hong Kong: a (British) lion and a (Chinese) dragon locked in battle.

Robert S. Elegant's family saga of the Sekloong Dynasty tells the story of the Chinese counterparts of the tai-pans. From the arrival in Hong Kong on May 28, 1900, of Mary Philippa Osgood, a naive English country girl and daughter of the director of the military band, until her ninetieth birthday on June 27, 1970, as the matron of the Sekloong Clan, Mary and her children directly experience China's history. They witness the fall of the Qing Dynasty, the First World War, the struggle between Communists and the Kuomintang, the Japanese invasion, the Second World War, Mao's revolution and his Cultural Revolution, and the effects these have upon Hong Kong: economic ups and downs, wars, pestilence, family feuds. The Sekloong

Clan functions as comprador for the largest trading house in Hong Kong, becomes its executive arm and connecting link to China and the Chinese. Practically bound entirely to the trading house, the Clan still exercises its obvious powers and manages to amass a vast fortune, both on the sly. The above constellation is also based on historical facts. Soon after their arrival in Hong Kong, European traders became dependent upon a number of clever Chinese for various services, be it as traders serving the Chinese population (always 90% of the total population), as contact persons to imperial traders, or as smugglers who brought opium in their junks, collected monies and bribed officials. This key position in trade, as well as politics, was often occupied by Eurasians. Because their mixed heritage was accepted by neither the Chinese nor the British, they had to establish their social position on the basis of practical talents. This passionate and permanent struggle for social recognition is also described very vividly in all three Hong Kong novels mentioned above.

Other novels available on the topic are not quite as good. In her autobiographical novel, Han Suyin tells the story of a love affair between a female Chinese physician and an English war correspondent during the times of the revolution in 1949. The author herself was born in China, the daughter of a Chinese and a Belgian. She studied and practised medicine and wrote numerous novels and other books on the new China, towards which she showed much sympathy.

John Gordon-Davis chose a more ambiguous revolution, the so-called Cultural Revolution after 1966, as the background for his novel. He tells the story of a British police officer during the troublesome year of 1967, when the hungry tiger briefly showed its claws in Hong Kong as well.

John Le Carré also set one of his counter-KGB spy stories in Hong Kong. Once again the protagonists battle with each other in the usual perfidious manner. And then, of course, there is still Richard Mason, who created an image of Hong Kong with his Suzie Wong that has little to do with reality. Those who search for the "World of Suzie Wong" in Hong Kong will do so in vain or have to use considerable imagination.

There are many more novels in English dealing with Hong Kong in 600 pages or more. Of these, Timothy Mo's *An Insular Possession* (London: Chatto & Windus 1986) stands out. It also takes a historical approach to the exciting founding years. Mo was born in Hong Kong in 1950, the son of an English mother and a Cantonese father. Today he works as a journalist in London.

At any rate, if you happen to have the time, do read Clavell's popular novels on Hong Kong. If you consider them as a kind of preparation for your journey, you are bound to enhance your perception of this city. Further literary references are available in the section "Useful Information", on page 140.

(Krücker)

Location, Structure and Landscapes

Even the name "Hong Kong" invites contradictions and discussions. The only thing clear is the fact that the English "Hong Kong" represents an effort to anglicize two Chinese, or rather Cantonese, syllables. A common explanation is that it was the Europeans with their large noses who first noticed the scent of exotic flowers and consequently named the 17th-century fishing village "Fragrant Harbour". The Cantonese thereupon translated it back to "heung kong tsuen".

Nothing against European noses, but Hong Kong was also referred to at one time as "Barren Island". In other words, not necessarily a place of exotic plantlife, which adds weight to yet another explanation. Apparently this region was known for the production of joss sticks during the Ming Dynasty (1369–1644). This would, of course, add another facet to the island's fragrance. After all, the production of joss sticks continues to be a traditional branch of industry in Hong Kong and Macao.

The North Chinese, from whom most official designations originate, obviously also have an official Chinese name for the area, namely *Xianggang*. It is supposed to refer to the pirate Xiang-gu (Hsiang-ku) and means "Xiang's Harbour". Strange that it should be Chinese civil servants, of all people, who remind us just what Hong Kong really was at the end of the 18th century: a pirate's nest!

However, an unravelling of the legend itself still does not clarify to which region the name actually applies. One can, in fact, differentiate between four separate areas: Hong Kong Island, Kowloon Peninsula, the New Territories with their mainland sectors, and the 235 other islands. Originally only the offshore island of Hong Kong belonged to the British Empire. This was a result of the First Opium War and the 1842 Treaty of Nanjing. Following the Peking Convention of 1860, the Chinese Empire also ceded the section of the Kowloon Peninsula up to today's Boundary Street and Stonecutters Island to the English. Kowloon, too, represents an anglicized version of a Chinese name. The area sketched above is that which was turned over to the British "for all time".

For security reasons, the British decided in 1898 to lease another 355 square miles for a period of 99 years. Since, without the aid of the Cantonese language, they were apparently at a loss for names, they simply called the newly-acquired lands "New Territories" and "Outlying Islands", by which they are still known today. According to military strategists, the acquisition of the new lands meant that it was possible to defend the

core of the colony more effectively –
a belief that was long untried and
ultimately proven erroneous when
the Japanese invaded. Nevertheless,
without this territory it would never
have been possible for 5 million
people to dwell in the city.

Location and Landscapes

The British crown colony lies at
27°17′ northern latitude, some 150
kilometres (93 miles) south of the
Tropic of Cancer, along mainland
China's southern coast. The greater
part of the 1,068 square kilometres
(412 square miles) of land is made up
of the New Territories (945 square
kilometres/365 square miles, including the islands). The northern borderline touches upon Guangdong
Province (capital city: Canton or
Guangzhou) in the People's
Republic of China.

The landscape is hilly to mountainous; the surface tends to be rocky.
Whereas Hong Kong Island is of vol-
canic origin, Kowloon's hills are made
up of granite and the mountains of
the New Territories (some of them as
much as 950 metres/3,117 feet in
height) are of crystalline rock.

Hong Kong Island

Even though Hong Kong was not
conceived of as a colonial settlement
from the start, its inhabitants always
had problems with space. The first
governors soon saw no alternative
but to launch reclamation projects: at
that time along the northern shores
of Hong Kong Island. Later on, the
filling in of swampy areas as well as

the reclamation of lands on both
shores of Kowloon and in the New
Territories followed. This process has
continued until the present day. Thus,
the once steep slopes of Victoria
Peak (named by the British in honour
of their queen, the 554 metres/1,818
feet of the peak dominate the northwestern corner of Hong Kong Island)
were ultimately levelled out enough
to allow the establishment of the first
permanent colonial settlement here.
It was first called Queen's Town and
its main thoroughfare, Queen's Road,
ran along the shoreline. Later the
settlement was renamed Victoria.

The earliest attempt by British
merchants to establish a settlement,
however, took place in Happy Valley.
It turned out to be a rather unhappy
choice of location because of the constant threat of malaria. A few villages
in the south of the island predated
the arrival of the British and were
later renamed by the new colonial
rulers. Lord Stanley served as
colonial undersecretary from 1841 to
1845 and Lord Aberdeen as foreign
secretary from 1841 to 1846.

Today, the western district is
characterized by the contrast between the traditional Chinese residential areas surrounding Man Mo
Temple and the first class addresses
in Central District where the western-
oriented business elite lives. Some-
where between all the glass structures one can still find a few remains
of colonial buildings. The richest of
the rich continue to live in their villas
along the slopes of the Peak, even
though the highrisers are ever
advancing in that direction.

It is already a well-known fact that Wanchai has lost its Suzie Wong flair and ceased being a sailor's haven. The nightclubs have either been supplemented with, or replaced by, good restaurants, theatres, sports arenas and establishments like the Hong Kong Arts Centre. Numerous department stores and smaller shops now compete with Tsimshatsui in Kowloon for customers.

Causeway Bay has a moving history behind it: it advanced from a marketplace in the times of the opium dealers to a residential area for the upper middle class. The shoreline is still dominated by the Causeway Bay Taiphoon Shelter with its many sampans serving as mini floating restaurants, but the tunnel now provides speedy access to the mainland, especially to the airport. No wonder then, that a number of luxury hotels have cropped up here recently.

The northeastern corner of the island is somewhat more remote. Industry and highrisers dominate here.

Highrisers also cast their shadows over the southern part of the island, but here there are no banks, office buildings or department stores. Instead, there are apartment houses, most of them housing former fishermen who moved off their junks to dry land. Outside of the few highrise districts, however, in the hills and along the beaches, Hong Kong appears in an entirely different light. During the week things go at a rural pace here. At weekends city dwellers go for walks along the beaches, in search of fresh air and enjoyment. Ocean Park is the main attraction.

Despite the fact that the actual number of boat people is steadily declining, there is still an impressive fleet anchored before Aberdeen. Many of these junks have never sailed out into the open sea. They are too small for the fishing industry or the coastal trade routes. So they

simply lie there side by side, tied up permanently as a landmark of the harbour city of Hong Kong.

Kowloon

Once a great emperor looked out over the peninsula to the hinterland and claimed he could see eight dragons. After all, every hill and mountain houses a dragon. An imperial official who wanted to humour his ruler looked at the emperor and said he could see nine dragons. According to Chinese tradition, the emperor himself was viewed as a dragon. Just as dragons populate Chinese legends, so do the legends themselves often dictate the course of history. Ever since the above event took place, the peninsula has been known as *gau lung* (nine dragons), or Kowloon in the anglicized version.

A hundred years ago a trip from the colony to Europe inevitably began with a sea voyage. Either one made the entire journey on board a sailing vessel or steamship, or one had to cross the harbour on the Star Ferry and then walk a few metres from the landing to the Orient Express to embark upon a journey overland lasting several weeks. Arriving passengers would get off the train, surrounded by porters, and make their way to the Peninsula Hotel.

Colonial opulence has since made way for sobriety and practicality. The clock tower is the only remaining relic of the old station. The new station, a low building of monstrous proportions, was built a few kilometres away on land reclaimed from the sea. But the number of exclusive hotels is steadily increasing and the "Peninsula" still has its guests picked up in a Rolls Royce. Department stores and business establishments now dominate Kowloon. And, of course, the means of transportation have changed: almost symbolically,

the airport's runways are stretching farther and farther into the harbour basin.

Nathan Road, named after Sir Matthew Nathan, who governed the crown colony from 1904 to 1907, disects Kowloon like a backbone. Thus it gives some form of order to the extraordinary mixture of luxury hotels, large and small shops, nightclubs and restaurants serving every kind of Asian food.

Also forming an integral part of Kowloon are the tiny apartments, often occupied by families of ten or more members and spanning four generations. While Hong Kong is considered to be one of the world's most populated areas, Mongkok in Kowloon is in turn the most densely populated part of Hong Kong. Up to 165,000 people live here per square kilometre. The working conditions in Kowloon's apartment house factories are as bad as the living conditions. It is here that Hong Kong's cheap goods and imitations are produced in day and night shifts.

New Territories (Mainland)

The New Territories actually begin in the middle of the city, on Boundary Street. A real "borderline", however, is nowhere to be seen: apartment houses and industrial complexes rise in uninterrupted rows. Smaller sectors closer to the border of the People's Republic, which were once tiny villages and then expanded into small towns during the 1960's, are now suburban areas with populations ranging from 250,000 to 500,000.

Once one has ventured beyond the fringes of the expanding city, one can still experience Chinese rural life. Farmers populate the hilly territory, where they raise pigs and poultry and even grow rice on terraces. Some of the steeper areas are not arable and left in their natural state. Thus rocky bushlands form yet another alternative to the hectic city life. Along the coast there are still numerous fishing villages where one can buy fish at the market and then take it over to a restaurant to be prepared. The most interesting markets are located in Lau Fau Shan and Tai Po.

Off the beaten track in the New Territories there are temples and traditional Chinese villages which are well worth visiting. Most of the temples pertain to the Buddhist-Taoist tradition; the Ching Chung Koon and Po Toi temples on Castle Peak (Tuen Mun), the Monastery of the Ten Thousand Buddhas in Shatin Valley or Tin-Hau Temple in Clearwater Bay are good examples. Seventeenth- and eighteenth-century life styles are recreated in the "walled villages" of Kam Tin.

Many of the region's inhabitants are Hakka. Their women are easy to recognize by the black clothing and wide, veiled hats they wear.

Finally, the New Territories provide Hong Kong's hard-working population with its favourite pastimes: the Shatin racecourse, the sandy beaches and nature park on Sai Kung Peninsula and, for the more affluent, the Clearwater Bay Golf and Country Club.

Offshore Islands

What a contrast to the ever pulsating city! The islands offer meadows, shrubs and trees, tiny bays and fishing villages, wide beaches and, above all, peace and quiet. Hong Kong's inhabitants only come here at weekends.

More than 200 islands and islets surround Hong Kong. These range in size from tiny, uninhabited islets to the island of Lantau, which covers an area twice as large as the original colony.

The islands are also hilly; Lantau Peak, for instance, reaches 935 metres (3,068 ft), therefore surpassing Victoria Peak. In previous times the islands were used as a refuge as well. No wonder then, that one can find monasteries of various denominations on a number of them.

The larger islands are easily accessible by ferry; otherwise, there is always the possibility of taking up passage on one of the fishing boats for a small fee.

The islanders still pursue traditional occupations: fishing, farming, handicrafts and retail trading. And a few even keep up an equally ancient tradition, namely smuggling. But it won't take long until the "giant" invades this territory as well. Exclusive hotels are being built and there are plans for an airport on Landau, which is to be connected to the mainland by a series of bridges and tunnels.

(Krücker)

Climate

Hong Kong lies in the Tropics. Its two seasons are dominated by monsoons: the summer monsoon, which brings hot and rainy weather with a high level of humidity from the southwest; and the winter monsoon coming in from the northeast, which produces a cool, dry climate.

The rainy season begins in mid-March. Temperatures rise steadily then, but so does the humidity. The sky is usually overcast and tropical showers occur with increasing frequency, occasionally replaced by a light drizzle. Summer nights do not offer much respite from the heat of the day.

Air conditioning in office buildings and hotels makes life more pleasant, but it is also a frequent source of colds. If you plan to travel to Hong Kong at this time of the year, you should bring along light cotton clothing as well as a sweater and jacket for use in air-conditioned rooms. Avoid clothing made of synthetic materials and don't forget a raincoat and an umbrella.

Typhoons are a common hazard during August and September of each year. In former times these were known to destroy half of the city; today, however, buildings are solidly constructed and the city has an effective warning system. Nevertheless, one should not underestimate the "big wind", as the Chinese call it, and remain in one's hotel during the time it blows through the city.

The best season of the year, from the end of September until December, begins with the advent of the dry monsoon. It remains warm but the humidity decreases, evenings cool down and the sky is bright blue. This is the best time to travel. All you need is light clothing and a thin sweater or jacket for the evenings.

Beginning mid-January, the weather becomes more fickle. Although temperatures still average around 15°C (59°F), it can get cool, windy and foggy. Up on the mountains temperatures can occasionally drop to 0°C (32°F). Your wardrobe should be selected accordingly.

(Jacobs)

Climatic Table: Hong Kong

Month	Daily highs		Daily lows		Hours of sunshine	Rainfall in mm	Rainy days per month
	°C	°F	°C	°F			
January	24	75	11	52	5	27	6
February	24	75	10	50	4	42	8
March	27	81	13	55	3	55	11
April	29	84	14	57	4	139	12
May	32	90	20	68	5	298	16
June	32	90	22	72	5	432	21
July	35	95	24	75	7	317	19
August	33	91	24	75	7	413	17
September	33	91	23	73	6	320	14
October	32	90	21	70	7	121	8
November	29	84	13	55	6	35	6
December	24	75	9	48	6	25	5

History

Hong Kong's history can be compared to that of a perpetual loser who finally takes first place by being persistent. The British foreign minister, Lord Palmerston, made the famous statement that he did not want this "barren island". The British navy and most traders were always after something they could not get and thus had to make do with Hong Kong as second choice. Hong Kong itself is solely the product of its harbour, which provided (and still provides) shelter from typhoons on the South China Sea and was a good location for the distribution of goods to South China as well as a stopover for traffic from North China.

The British described Hong Kong as a "peculiar colony", because it was intended as a "factory", or trading post, rather than a settlement. This meant that its economic role was dominant from the very start. But then, the British Empire had a number of such contracted harbours; so why was Hong Kong so much more successful than, for instance, Aden? Though it may sound somewhat paradoxical at first, one possible explanation for this phenomenon lies in the fact that Europeans and Chinese had such great problems with each other. These, however, were usually settled in a constructive manner and not by military force. Europeans did, of course, arrive in eastern Asia with their usual arrogant attitudes and laden down with cannons. But in China they were confronted by a self-confident people whose rulers had the same feelings of superiority as their European counterparts.

During the 16th century only the Portuguese had a worldwide net of trading posts. In 1557 they were permitted to settle in Macao, from where they established relations with the Chinese and Japanese. The Chinese, however, showed little inclination to deal with those whom they considered to be barbarians and "foreign devils". Their society was entirely self-sufficient and they felt no need for the rough wares the foreigners offered in exchange for their silk, tea and silver. In order not to become "infected" by the foreign elements, trading activity was restricted to Canton, and even there to a specific area outside the city walls.

The British, on the other hand, were more interested in their colonial territories in India than the Far East and thus allowed the East India Company to monopolize trade. This slowed trading down for many years, but also made it easy to control. It wasn't until 1833, after the East India Company lost its monopoly for the trade with the colonies, that the situation began to change, thus initiating the process that was to lead to the development of Hong Kong. The independent traders, who had managed to break down the British monopoly, were now keen to encroach upon that of the Chinese.

Foreign traders were only permitted to remain in their trading posts near Canton for five months of the year. Their partners were traders organized under and controlled by the Chinese Co-Hong, who did not enjoy a very high reputation in Chinese society but still dictated the prices and volume of trade to the Europeans. Payment had to be made in silver bars because the Chinese were not interested in English cotton fabric, produced in the mills of Yorkshire and Lancashire. To add to the European traders' chagrin, Britain was just evolving as a nation of tea drinkers and tea was solely cultivated in impenetrable Japan and in China. Numerous smugglers attempted to bring seeds or seedlings to India or some other British territory, but this was not accomplished until some later unknown date.

The first chapter in the history of Hong Kong can thus be summarized under the title "tea". The second chapter was not so harmless. As the British were no longer prepared to pay in silver for their ever growing demand in tea, they turned to an alternative that was to shape the destiny of China and Hong Kong for the following 150 years. That alternative was opium.

Opium had been used by the Chinese for medicinal purposes as early as the Tang era (618–907), but it wasn't until the 17th century, with the introduction of tobacco, that it also became popular to smoke it. Though only some 200 crates containing 65 kilogrammes (143 pounds) were actually imported in 1729, the Chinese emperor nevertheless passed an edict that same year prohibiting the use of the drug. By 1780, however, imports had increased dramatically and at the beginning of the 19th century traders from Britain and other countries were importing the forbidden drug into China in order to exchange it directly for tea or to sell it for silver with which they could in turn purchase tea.

In 1825 the Chinese balance of trade made an about turn: whereas previously China had acquired silver from the sale of tea and silk, it was now experiencing an unprecedented drain of the precious metal. As the value of silver coins was directly dependent upon the metal itself, a wave of inflation soon followed and exacerbated China's existing problems – health hazards caused by the use of the drug and corruption within the imperial administration. This situation came to a head during the 1830's. The British wanted to increase their trade, which meant selling more opium. This was only possible, however, if the monopoly of the Co-Hongs in Canton could be broken. The Chinese, in turn, wanted to stabilize their economy again, which had been disrupted by the "foreign poison".

At that time, the most vehement supporter of a strict prohibition policy was the imperial official Lin Zexu (Lin Tse-hsu); at the beginning of 1839 he was sent to Canton as imperial representative. He confiscated all of the opium stored in Canton and, in June of that year, had 19,179 crates and 2,119 sacks of the drug burned. Military tension ensued. The British foreign minister demanded financial reparation as well as a settlement area for the protection of British traders.

Palmerston had much more in mind than the island of Hong Kong: his goal was to open all of China for trade with the West and to establish trading posts at five or six harbour towns along the coast for that purpose. Seeking a suitable location for the establishment of a defendable base both for trade and the navy, most military personnel and merchants had their eyes on the island of Zhoushan (Chusan), rather than Hong Kong. Zhoushan's position just off Shanghai was very similar to that of Hong Kong in relation to Canton, but the former would have opened up a much greater part of China for trading activity.

The result of the first part of the First Opium War was that on January 20, 1841, the Mandarin Qishan (Kishen), Lin Zexu's successor, and Captain Charles Elliot, representative of the British Crown, signed the Chuanbi Convention, which provided for reparation payments and the transfer of Hong Kong. Without awaiting the response from the two royal heads of state, Commodore Sir J. J. Gordon Bremer of the Royal Navy took possession of Hong Kong at what became known as Possession Point on January 26, 1841.

However, both representatives had only succeeded in incurring the displeasure of their respective sovereigns and were duly recalled. Elliot's successor, Sir Henry Pottinger, had instructions to open up harbours on the coast of mainland China for trade. Taking advantage of the favourable fall winds, he led the British fleet northward for renewed armed conflict.

As it has been amply recorded in history, the cannon boats before the capital city of Nanjing ultimately caused the emperor to intercede. On August 29, 1842, he agreed to sign the Treaty of Nanjing, a treaty which has always been considered by the Chinese to have been entirely one-sided. China had to pay 21 million silver dollars in compensation for the opium and war damages; the seaports of Shanghai, Ningbo, Xiamen, Fuzhou and Canton had do be opened; and the island of Hong Kong ceded to the British Crown.

The treaty was ratified by British Parliament on June 26, 1843, and Sir Henry Pottinger took up office as first governor of the Crown Colony.

Other than the Hong Kong lobby – made up of a few local traders and opium smugglers – no one was actually satisfied with this solution. Elliot had thought that Hong Kong would take over Canton's monopoly in the field of foreign trade, but the simultaneous opening of the seaports on the mainland ultimately resulted in Shanghai's quick rise in economic importance. Once again, Hong Kong had to make do with a mere second place. This explains why the independent seaport of Hong Kong, which was open to all nations (including up-and-coming Americans), emerged initially as an entrepôt for shipping lines between Europe, Southeast Asia and the Chinese coast.

Hong Kong's inhabitants had numerous problems to contend with from the start. The new colony lacked sufficient funds to take care of public concerns such as road construction, health services and the maintenance of a military and police force. The greater part of its earnings came from land leases, which meant that the government in London had to make continuous payments to bolster its budget. This, of course, did not do much for the popularity of the "barren island" over on the British Isles.

The population of Hong Kong grew dramatically during the first ten years of British rule but then the increase slowed down considerably. The population of the colony was primarily made up of mainland Chinese who came to Hong Kong as labourers. This early framework of the population has remained constant in the city until the present day. Over 90 per cent of the inhabitants were Chinese who remained fairly independent of the British colonial government and lived according to their own customs and laws. They established secret societies and an internal economic system. Soon, the richest inhabitants of Hong Kong were Chinese. In contrast to Macao, miscegenation hardly took place here.

Opium remained the primary object of trade in Hong Kong for many decades; the differences between Britain and China were far from having been solved by the Treaty of Nanjing. The Second Opium War, which lasted from 1856 to 1860, further weakend the unstable Qing dynasty. As a result of the 1860 Peking Convention, the Crown Colony received the peninsula of Kowloon. The British governor wanted to relocate all of his troops there, but the establishment of the legation sector in Peking and the strengthened position of foreigners in the open seaports reduced Hong Kong's importance in trade between Europe and China.

Actually, it was the Chinese in Hong Kong who maintained the colony economically. Their ever increasing numbers created demands, and in addition Hong Kong progressively developed into the main port of departure for Chinese emigrating to Southeast Asia and America. This gave rise to a thriving trade with Chinese communities abroad which, by the way, continues to play an important role in the economy today. Trade goods basically remained the same: opium, tea, silk, salt, sugar, rice and rattan.

At this time a shipbuilding and marine equipment industry began to develop as well. But Hong Kong's economic dilemma also remained as acute as ever. Since the colony was a free port and therefore could hardly charge customs taxes, it had to draw its income primarily from land leases; and land had always been a scarce commodity.

Towards the end of the 19th century Hong Kong was peripherally drawn into the imperialistic ambitions of the European powers. The French, Russians and Germans wanted to extend their dominion in the Far East, at the cost of the Chinese wherever possible. The United States also embarked upon an imperialistic venture with its conquest of the Philippines in 1898. Thus it was the rivalry between colonial powers – especially fear of a possible French attack – that prompted the British to expand their territory in Hong Kong.

Consequently, on July 1, 1898, they leased the New Territories for a period of 99 years.

The Chinese empire was about to collapse. Although the Boxer Rebellion of 1900 was, above all, a reaction to foreign exploitation of China, it was also directed against the despotic imperial government. Most of the Chinese in Hong Kong took sides with the reformers. Among them was the future architect of the first Chinese republik, Sun Yat-sen, who grew up in Hong Kong and graduated from the Chinese Medical College there in 1892. The reformers also opposed the opium trade, which led to a marked reduction in the consumption of the drug following the turn of the century. Opium dens were closed down in 1909. In order to compensate for some two million HK-Dollars in lost income, the government levied a tax on alcohol, tobacco and perfume. This special tax is still imposed today and the only exception in an otherwise duty-free economy.

The 1911 revolution, which overthrew the Manchu dynasty, hardly affected Hong Kong as the latter was far removed from events in China, and the southern merchants supported the new rulers in Peking anyway.

The First World War had no direct effect on Hong Kong either, but the economy of the Crown Colony ultimately felt some of the changes. European influence in the Far East, especially that of the Germans, Russians (following the 1917 October Revolution) and British, decreased. The Japanese, on the other hand, gained in power and influence as they expanded their territory into Korea and China. At the same time, an economic crisis had developed in London which was eventually to engulf the pound sterling economy worldwide.

The 1920's and 1930's also brought severe economic problems to Hong Kong that could only be solved by a severance from Great Britain in favour of a process of internationalization.

World War Two brought on another recession as well as countless waves of mainland Chinese refugees and the organization of a Hong Kong volunteer corps. Nevertheless, Hong Kong could not be held militarily. On December 8, 1941, shortly after the attack on Pearl Harbor, the Japanese invaded the New Territories by land and bombarded the few fighter-planes on the ground at Kai Tak Airport. Five days later the defending forces withdrew to the island of Hong Kong with the Japanese hot on their heels. Although they made a desperate stand, the defenders finally capitulated on Christmas Day of that year.

The Japanese occupation authorities sent 7,000 prisoners of war to forced labour camps in Japan; most of those sent never returned. They also drove out about a million of Hong Kong's inhabitants, reducing the population to 600,000. In 1945 the American Air Force attacked the Japanese positions and the Navy blockaded the harbour; the Japanese surrendered August 14.

At the Yalta Conference in 1945, the Allies divided up the world into spheres of influence. The Americans proposed that Hong Kong be returned to the Chinese, whom they considered to be the victors in the Far East (China was not represented at the conference). But the British and Hong Kong Chinese simply ignored this suggestion and quickly set up a new administration following the war. China could hardly interfere as it was embroiled in a civil war.

This internal conflict between communists and the Kuomintang (the latter retreated to Taiwan in 1949) brought numerous refugees to Hong Kong. The population climbed from 600,000 in 1945 to 2,360,000 just five years later. In October 1, 1949, Mao Tse-tung proclaimed the People's Republic of China in Peking. While the U. S. A. reacted with an economic and political boycott, Great Britain chose to recognize the People's Republic by February of 1950, probably as a gesture towards the Communist Party calculated to help secure the status of Hong Kong.

However, the differences between the former Allied powers finally led to the Cold War in Europa. In Asia, on the other hand, the conflict turned into a hot one. The Korean War (1950–1953) and the war in Vietnam also drew Hong Kong into the resulting political and economic maelstrom. Nevertheless, the city's economic framework had changed considerably and thus could continue to supply the Western contenders in these wars as well as to provide a recreation area for the soldiers (the "world of Suzie Wong" was a product of the 1950's).

Once again, though, it was the Chinese who saved Hong Kong's economy after World War II. The countless refugees brought many problems with them, but they also provided valuable labour. Of course, a good many of those who fled from the communists also had capital or industrial know-how. Most of them came from Shanghai, which led to a renewal in Hong Kong of the old rivalry between the Shanghaians and Cantonese. Finally, the ever second-best Hong Kong had become a winner.

The Chinese completely changed the economic structure of Hong Kong. In addition to the free trade, they began to set up a productive industry. At first this was dominated by textiles, then plastic wares and, after 1959, electronics. The work force grew from 64,000 in 1947 to 590,000 in 1970, a figure which did not even take into account the numerous small and independent subcontracting businesses. Beginning after the mid-1950's, Hong Kong was able to secure a place for itself alongside Taiwan, South Korea and Singapore in the explosive economic growth of East Asia. It did this by using cheap labour to convert imported raw materials into finished export goods. Today, it is ranked as one of the "four small tigers" following in the footsteps of Japan.

The waves of refugees coupled with miserable working conditions led to increasing social tensions. In 1953, when the number of refugees had reached a peak, a fire broke out in one of the slum areas and left 53,000 people homeless. For the first time in its history, the administration in Hong Kong launched a social programme under which, within a period of fifteen years, more than a million people were moved into subsidized apartments. Since then numerous blocks of huge apartment houses have shot up, seemingly overnight.

Still, the people continue to live in cramped conditions. Despite the fact that almost half of the population now lives in such apartment complexes and both housing and reclamation projects are going on continually, the urgent need for living quarters has hardly abated.

The administration also set up rudimentary labour regulations based on European models, and improved its health service as well as the educational system. The opening of the Chinese University in 1963 was a symbol of the new policy.

Relations with the huge neighbour, the People's Republic, went on in a quiet manner. Hong Kong needed provisions, energy and water, and Peking, an open door towards the West.

Only once, at the height of the Cultural Revolution (1966–69), did social unrest spill over the otherwise very tightly controlled border. In May of 1967, workers and taxi drivers declared a strike. Demonstrators took to the streets, supported by representatives from Peking who held high positions in the Bank of China and the local office of the Xinhua press association. Cars and buses went up in flames; police and military struck back brutally. Even though the planned general strike never took place, a state of unrest continued until December. It wasn't until 1981, after the change in the political climate in the People's Republic and just prior to the negotiations over Hong Kong's future, that the Peking government officially voiced its regret to the administration in Hong Kong concerning the events outlined above.

The 1967 social tensions clearly showed the extent of the People's Republic's influence in Hong Kong. Nevertheless, Peking has always needed Hong Kong as a doorway to the rest of the world. This applies even more so to the present reformist government. Thus there is good reason to hope that the so typically Chinese arrangement – the synthesis of contradictions – will persist under the new conditions following the year 1997.   (Krücker)

The Future has already begun: What happens in 1997?

When Margaret Thatcher became involved in negotiations over Hong Kong's future, she first had to recognize the discrepancies between theory and the real situation there. In 1982 she had declared that the New Territories were negotiable but Hong Kong was to remain British. A glance at any map would have made it clear to her that there was no room for boundaries on Boundary Street.

The People's Republic could have swallowed the two remaining colonial bastions of Hong Kong and Macao a long time ago. Following the wave of decolonization in Africa during the 1960's, public opinion throughout the world would certainly not have supported the colonial powers. It is questionable whether the latter would even have faced up to China at the time. During the so-called "Carnation Revolution" in 1974, the new Portuguese government even offered to give up Macao to the Chinese voluntarily, but the administration in Peking declined with thanks. Chinese remain Chinese, regardless of where they may be living. As far as they are concerned, there is only one China: whatever regime may be ruling a certain area at the time is only of secondary importance. Only the Europeans maintain the illusion that they have actually exercized power in Hong Kong. Whatever political phases the Communist Party in Peking may have gone through, its policy towards Hong Kong and Macao has remained constant. The Chinese tend to think on a long-term basis.

Rather than the tumultuous Cultural Revolution, it is China's current economic policy, adopted following the changes in Chinese politics after 1978, that has contributed towards a shift in the status of Hong Kong and Macao. Previously, trade with or through Hong Kong and Macao had to remain secret. The connections with capitalism as well as contacts with Taiwan, Japan, the U.S. and Europe simply did not fit into the local political scenery of the times. The fact that the owner of the largest gambling establishment in Macao was none other than a certain delegate of the Political Consultative Conference of the People's Republic, where gambling is strictly forbidden, was only whispered about secretly. Today Peking conducts an official foreign policy and strives to adapt to the conditions on the open world market. Consequently, the time is also appropriate to include Hong Kong and Macao into this new policy and to profit from both their location and know-how. As early as 1979, just one year after the political shift in Peking began, Deng Xiaoping had let it slip through secret diplomatic channels that the Chinese government intended to take over the colony in 1997. If the formula "one country – two systems" can function at all, then only in China, which has acquired its pragmatism in the course of its 5,000-year-old history.

The initial positions and interests of both parties were clearly discernible. Great Britain wanted to terminate the lease agreements. It also wanted to keep the free harbour open for world trade. But, above all else, the British did not want further Chinese immigration to their homeland, especially after having to deal with a flood of immigrants from its other former colonies. The People's Republic, on the other hand, was interested in assuming political control over Hong Kong and using it as a main base for its foreign trade. At the same time, however, they wanted to prevent the infiltration of capitalism and Hong Kong's life style into its own territory. Hong Kong's inhabitants, who had the least say in these negotiations, most definitely wanted to maintain this life style as well as their political system. A complete takeover by the People's Republic would undoubtedly have led to an exodus of both people and capital. As the inhabitants of Hong Kong are primarily Chinese, they are not so much concerned about the government itself, which they have also tended to ignore in the past, just as long as they can continue to pursue their favourite activity: making money.

Even before serious negotiations had begun, Peking brought about a new element in its economic policy: special economic zones. These are located across the borders from those Chinese territories presently dominated by a capitalist system. Shenzhen, the most important one, lies due north of Hong Kong; Zhuhai is to the west of Macao; and Shantou and Xiamen face Taiwan. Here the capitalist system is being tried out in the form of joint-ventures without purposely changing the existing social structures. At the present time it is more difficult to travel within the People's Republic, e. g. from Canton to Shenzhen, than from Hong Kong to said zone. Numerous Chinese have already invested in Shenzhen. With a permanent visa they travel to the People's Republic each morning to work and then return to Hong Kong's somewhat sweeter life in the evenings.

After two years of negotiations, an agreement was finally written up on September 26, 1984, and signed in Peking on December 19 of that same year. It basically makes a compromise between the British Commonwealth and the People's Republic, which takes into consideration the economic developments outlined above. It provides that the entire territory be returned to China by July 1, 1997, but that it retain its present political and economic structures for the next fifty years as a "special territory". The present administration is to remain as it is for the greater part, Hong Kong is to continue as a free port with an independent customs sector and the Hong Kong Dollar is to be retained as convertible currency. No one is to be expropriated, fiscal autonomy is to remain in the hands of the municipal authorities, profits need not be transferred to Peking and both goods and capital are to circulate freely. The governor is to be replaced as head of the municipal council by an official either nominated in Peking or elected by the local population. So far, only lower positions in the administration have been open to elections in Hong Kong. Neither Great Britain nor the Communist Party in Peking seems to be presently interested in a more democratic future for Hong Kong.

And just what will the economic future be like? It will depend not only upon Hong Kong's, but the entire world's confidence in the development of the Chinese reform policies, as well as the successful integration of elements from a free-enterprise system into the socialist economy of the third largest nation on earth. Since the signing of the agreement there has been no marked outflow of capital registered. Of course larger concerns have taken precautions and set up alternatives in other regions. Some individuals have undoubtedly procured a Canadian or Australian passport, just to be on the safe side.

On the whole, however, these seem to be no more than precautionary measures. As long as Peking continues to respect (or make use of) Hong Kong's economic freedom, it seems quite likely that the latter will maintain its advantageous position over the ever-blossoming Shanghai for a few more decades.

Nevertheless, from the mainland Chinese point of view Hong Kong continues to take second place. The principle of "one country – two systems" applies primarily to another long-term objective: Taiwan. The government in Peking will do all it can to guarantee the success of the Hong Kong experiment in order to reunite the nation and demonstrate its superiority over the separatist brethren of the Kuomintang over on Taiwan. Even if it should take another hundred years.   *(Krücker)*

The Economy

Actually, Hong Kong has remained just what it was 140 years ago: an important entrepôt for world trade. The dimensions, rather than the functions, have changed. A few figures will prove the point: with its 5.5 million inhabitants the city holds a mere 0.1 per cent of the world's population; but they control a full one per cent of world trade, i. e. ten times their theoretical share. Industry which began to emerge after World War II has since expanded to some 47,000 businesses; these export 95 per cent of their products to more than 160 countries throughout the world. On

the other hand, Hong Kong's almost complete dependency on imports in essential sectors like energy, water and food supplies has also remained unchanged.

"Free enterprise" has been Hong Kong's economic philosophy from the very start, and continues to be so to this very day. Its economic policy has always been based on minimal interference from the government. With few exceptions, permits for commercial enterprises are not required. There are no bottom limits for the capital resources of an enterprise, no guidelines for reinvestment, no export limitations, hardly any customs duties, almost no social contributions and low taxes. In 1958, at a time when a socially-inclined economy was establishing itself "at home", Hong Kong became almost entirely autonomous. Great Britain only represented Hong Kong in matters of foreign policy, the young queen remaining the nominal head of state. As far as the economy was concerned, however, the distant government refrained from interfering. It simply had to accept reality.

With a remarkable admixture of state-controlled planning and private investment and execution, Hong Kong managed to create an unsurpassed infrastructure for both people and enterprises. The harbour has been the dominant area of economic development for 140 years; today it is the world's third largest container port. Kai Tak Airport caters to more than 30 international airlines and has highly modern passenger and freight service facilities; but it only has one runway. Lack of available space continues to limit Hong Kong's progress. For years now, the administration has been conferring to discuss plans for the transfer of the airport to the island of Lantau. Communications systems in Hong Kong are up to the most modern standards and thus connect it effectively with the rest of the world.

The infrastructure of the inner city is also based on the fusion of state planning and private execution. Be it the harbour tunnel or the under-ground (MTR), it is private investors who provide the funds for, and manage, public transport, and that at very low prices which have remained stable over the decades and still produce profits.

Much of Hong Kong's success since World War II has been due to its unique situation: small and therefore easy to manage, Hong Kong became an attractive proposition for people active in an area where the greater nations (the People's Republic of China and the countries of Southeast Asia) had reached a state of economic stagnation. Above all, however, Hong Kong's success is an Asian success, because the Chinese also control its economy. Of the 130,000 business enterprises in the city, only 2,000 are foreign concerns.

The historical situation and geographical location also determined from the very start the type of goods which would be produced. Hong Kong has specialized almost entirely in light industry and consumer goods. It all began with textiles and to this day about 30% of the businesses and 25% of the employees are still involved in this branch of industry. As far as the export of textiles is concerned, however, Hong Kong has had to sign agreements with numerous countries limiting the amount of low-priced goods it supplies. Today a permit is required for exporting textiles.

Synthetics and plastics also figured from the start and presently make up about ten per cent of total pro-

are not so well known around the world because they are of mainly regional significance. These include a food-processing industry, a chemical industry and, above all, a flourishing, high-capacity paper-processing, printing and publishing industry. Innumerable newspapers and magazines are printed in Hong Kong and sent to countries throughout East and Southeast Asia.

In recent times Hong Kong's watchmaking and jewellery businesses have gained in importance. Based on the number of watches exported, Hong Kong is already the number one in the world; in terms of value, however, it is still in third place. Its reputation as a production and trade centre for jewellery is rapidly approaching that of its major competitor, Tokyo.

duction. The toy industry plays a major role, but it is in this sector primarily that the transfer to joint-ventures in the special economic zone of Shenzen in the People's Republic is taking place.

Hong Kong experienced a veritable boom with the advent of electronics. Just about every conceivable electric and electronic part or finished product is made here, including transistors, semiconductors, pocket calculators, radios, televisions, electronic toys and other gadgets as well as highly modern computers. This is by far the fastest growing branch of Hong Kong's ever expanding industry.

Hong Kong is also the base for a number of economic activites which

As an international seaport and commercial centre, Hong Kong obviously ranks among the great seafaring nations. More than 1,500 ships with over 57 million tonnes capacity ply the seas for shipping companies based in Hong Kong. By cooperating with shipping companies in the People's Republic of China, practically a non-seafaring nation with a rising export quota, some of the major shipowners in Hong Kong have managed to circumvent the uncertainties plaguing the transport business, especially in the case of supertankers. Another firm in the transport business, the Hong Kong-based (and privately-owned, of course) Cathay Pacific Airways, also registered a continuing growth rate in both passenger and freight services during the 1980's.

In 1985, Hong Kong was able to register a slight plus in its foreign trade balance for the first time. With the exception of a brief setback during the worldwide recession at the beginning of the 1980's, foreign sales have augmented steadily. As a free port and "doorway to China", Hong Kong's importance in the foreign trade sector is also increasing markedly. About 45 per cent of the import and export goods are merely stored in the seaport for further shipping.

The United States and China are the main export destinations, receiving about 30% of total exports each (1985). Japan stands in third place with a mere 4.3%, followed by Great Britain with 4.2% and West Germany with 4.1%. Hong Kong's import quotas make clear the dependence upon the Chinese "hinterlands": the People's Republic leads the chart, providing 25.6% of Hong Kong's total imports. It is followed by Japan with 23.2%, the United States with 9.5% and Singapore with 4.9%. Then come Great Britain, South Korea and West Germany. Great Britain continues to import more goods from Hong Kong than it exports to Hong Kong.

As a modern trade centre, Hong Kong also had to expand its financial sector substantially, which it did with great success. Today Hong Kong is the world's third largest finance centre. More than 140 banks with over 1,400 branches hold city permits; 35 of them are local institutions. In addition to these there are numerous insurance companies, pension funds and investment funds. Hong Kong, with its peculiar semi-national administration, does not have its notes issued at a central bank. This is done by two private banks, the Hong Kong and Shanghai Banking Corporation and the Chartered Bank. Only coins are minted by the government.

The above is an obvious indication that the state does not interfere much in matters of finance. All it does in this sector is pressure private enterprises in a certain direction without, however, actually being able to force them in any way. This was the case, for instance, with the merging of the four separate stock markets.

The number of gainfully employed in Hong Kong rose consistently during the 1970's and 1980's. It is only in very recent times that a temporary ceiling has been reached here. Close to 48 per cent of the 2.6 million inhabitants are gainfully employed. The unemployment rate is about four per cent. In the last few years there has been a clear tendency among the younger inhabitants to prolong the duration of their education or training. Most of the gainfully employed work in production industries; but those in the service sector already take second place, before office employees. Nearly ten per cent, or 250,000, of the gainfully employed are involved in trade. Agriculture hardly plays a role in these statistics: in Hong Kong a mere 32,000 people make a living as farmers or fishermen (1.2 per cent of the gainfully

Agriculture

In comparison to trade and industry, agriculture plays a minor role. Since only nine per cent of the total land area is arable, the five million inhabitants of the city depend upon imports from the People's Republic of China for approximately three quarters of their food requirements. Only as far as fish and seafood supplies are concerned is Hong Kong fairly self-sufficient. Rice production in the crown colony has decreased markedly since the mid-1950's, being progressively replaced by more profitable vegetable cultivation. The land area under rice cultivation thus shrank from close to 25,000 acres to a mere 740 acres. Rice is currently imported from the People's Republic, Thailand and the Philippines. The main vegetables cultivated are cabbage, beans, pumpkins, cucumber, aubergines, carrots, spinach, tomatoes and leeks. In addition one finds sweet potatoes, peanuts, soya beans und sugar cane. Mandarins, lemons, bananas, guavas and lychees are grown in orchards.

As pork and poultry are the main ingredients of Chinese cooking, many of the farmers in the New Territories have opted to raise pigs, ducks and geese. The number of chickens, about seven million, is considerably higher than the human population. It is also here that one comes across the large tanks in which freshwater fish, primarily carp, are reared.

In Hong Kong the fishing business is much more important than farming. Some 4,700 fishing boats with less than 100 tonnes-capacity, four fifths of them motorized, ply the surrounding seas and provide both households and restaurants with close to 200,000 tonnes of fresh seafood each year.

Timber does not figure in the economy as the sole purpose of reforestation programmes is to protect the karstic hill regions.

(Krücker)

employed or 0.58 per cent of the population).

The highest wages are earned in the construction business, but both those employed in the printing industry and artisans also do quite well. Lowest wages are still being paid in the textiles industry. Even though social services are currently regulated by a number of laws, these are not always enforceable and usually prove to be insufficient. For the greater part, health insurance and retirement pension have to be secured by the individuals themselves and their families.

(Krücker)

Transport

If all of Hong Kong's 300,000 auto-mobiles, 12,000 buses, 70,000 lorries and 25,000 motorcycles were to be on the road at one time, they would occupy the entire 1,500 kilometres (932 miles) of road network. Even though the number of motorized vehicles is fairly low on a per capita basis, the situation outlined above clearly illustrates Hong Kong's traffic problem. While private vehicles congest the streets and pollute the air substantially, they still play only a minor role in day to day transportation of the population.

Faced with the necessity of providing transport for the people in this overcrowded city, the administration, in conjunction with private initiative and investment, established a public transport system which is not only very efficient, but also cheap and still profitable. More than ten million people make use of the Hong Kong public transport system on an average day.

Star Ferry: undoubtedly the oldest means of public transport in Hong Kong. It was introduced in 1870 and today ten ships cruise back and forth between terminals at the tip of Kowloon and the Central District on Hong Kong Island itself; services operate from 6.30 am to 11.30 pm. Besides being an absolute "must" in a visitor's itinerary, a cruise on the Star Ferry provides an ideal opportunity for taking photographs of Kowloon or the Island.

Wallah Wallah: when the crew of the Star Ferry go off duty, the owners of these sampans, or small junks, take on passengers for crossings. Their crafts can, of course, also be hired during the day, but this is not exactly cheap.

Island Ferries: ferries to islands like Lamma, Lantau, Cheung Chau or Peng Chau dock at piers located between the Star Ferry Pier and Macao Ferry Terminal. The names of the islands are printed on signboards; clocks show the next departure times. Most of the ferries operate on an hourly basis.

Trams: the old tramcar clatters along 30 kilometres (19 miles) of tracks on the northern side of the island, back and forth between Kennedy Town and Shaukeiwan. Plans have apparently been made to close it down, but so far it continues to form an integral part of the street scenery in the old colonial area. It started its services in 1904; the double-deckers, which obtained a solid roof in exchange for their previous sailcloth coverings in 1923, were introduced in 1912. The fare is always the same, regardless of the distance covered; coins to the value of the fare are simply dropped into a box next to the driver when one gets off again. Be sure to have the right amount in coins with you as change is not provided.

Peak Tram: a funicular has been making the 399-metre (1,300 ft) climb from the valley to the station on the Peak since 1888. The green cars, in which a seat had to remain permanently reserved for the governor until 1949, make five stops along the way. They are connected by a cable so that the downhill cars help to pull the uphill ones. Even though it has to surmount an incredibly steep incline, the Peak Tram has never been involved in an accident. Its services were only interrupted by World War II and once in 1966 during heavy monsoon rain. It operates every 20 minutes between 7am and midnight and covers the distance of 1.4 kilometres in eight minutes.

Buses: you don't have to go to London to catch a ride on a red double-decker bus. The "Kowloon Motor Bus Company" operates such vehicles in Kowloon and the New Territories, and the "China Motor Bus Company" has them rolling on the streets of Hong Kong Island. Both companies make use of the harbour tunnel. Fares vary according to destination; prices within the city can be gleaned from the rotating signboards in front of the bus. The fare is dropped into a box next to the driver when getting on the bus; as in the case of trams, no change is given. Most of the drivers do not speak English, so it is advisable to check your route and the corresponding bus number on a schedule available from the Hong Kong Tourist Association.

Airport Buses: two bus lines operate regularly between the airport and a string of major hotels. Line 200 serves Hong Kong Island and line 201 goes to Kowloon. Of course, the buses can also be used for the return trip; they depart about every fifteen minutes. Please bear in mind that during rush hour buses from Kowloon to the airport can take up to 45 minutes and those from Central even an hour and a half.

Minibuses: the beige minibuses have fixed routes, but they will stop anywere passengers might want to get on or off. Give the driver a clear signal to stop. Most of the buses, however, will only bear route designations in Chinese, so that one has to inform oneself beforehand about the desired route and know one's way around the city somewhat.

Rickshas are popular motifs for tourist, but only seldom used as a means of transportation.

Underground (MTR, Mass Transit Railway): this is Hong Kong's newest and fastest transport system. There are three lines: one from the east; one from the western part of the New Territories to Kowloon and then over to the Island; and one that runs along Hong Kong's north side, from Chai Wan to Central. Once you have managed to find an entrance to the Underground – not always easy because of the innumerable neon signs – you should check for the fare for your proposed destination on the signboard. Then you go over to one of the automats displaying the required fare and pull a coded plastic card (automats take only coins). This card is used to pass the ticket barrier and should be kept until arrival as it will be needed to exit again. Here the fare will be automatically checked; should you have pulled a card with insufficient fare, you can pay the excess fare at one of the counters without being fined. If you plan to use the subway repeatedly, you should purchase a multiple-fare card. This will not be any cheaper, but it will spare you the trouble of having to have the right change and stand in long queues in front of the automats. Inquire at the Hong Kong Tourist Association or at the MTR stations about special tourist cards.

Railway: Hong Kong's new train station is located in Hung Hom, in the vicinity of the entrance to the Harbour Tunnel. Local electric services operate from here to the New Territories, and all the way to Lo Wu on the border with the People's Republic of China. However, only those holding a visa for the People's Republic can travel this far. Border clearance takes place just at the end of the platform. In 1986 some 19 million passengers embarked or disembarked at Lo Wu Station, most of them Hong Kong Chinese on their way to visit relatives in southern China.

A further 1.8 million travellers also used the non-stop train from Hong Kong to Guangzhou (Canton) in 1986; this departs four times daily from the same station. Here, too, one has to have a visa for the People's Republic.

Those who do not plan to cross the border have to get off the local train at Sheung Shui Station at the very latest. It takes about a half hour to get there. Local trains operate at intervals of about 10 to 15 minutes.

Taxi: the cabs are all of the same colour: red body with a grey roof and a white taxi sign on top. All are equipped with a taximeter and required by law to use it. Taxi rides are not particularly expensive, as long as one does not use the Harbour Tunnel. In the latter case, the driver can charge double the amount of the regular tunnel toll.

The taxis in the New Territories are all green with white tops. They are also cheaper than on the Island.

Helicopter: should you be in a hurry or just in a mood to see Hong Kong from above, then you can hire a helicopter. A helicopter will take a maximum of five passengers; the price remains the same whether it be full or not. Information is available at the Hong Kong Tourist Association or Heliservices Hong Kong Ltd.
(Krücker)

Flora and Fauna

The discovery came as a surprise to us, as we thought we already knew Hong Kong quite well: on the southern slope of a hill in the New Territories, one of the very few still in its natural state, we found a handful of banana trees standing between a number of camphor trees and blossoming bushes. With the help of an interpreter, the farmer let us know that he could even harvest the wild bananas once a year. They were of the small kind, which do not look as smooth and yellowish-green as the ones found in the supermarket, but taste absolutely delicious.

It is estimated that there are more than 2,500 species of **plants** in Hong Kong, some of which were imported at some time or another and others which are endemic. Primarily one will find camphor trees, pine and banyans, as well as eucalyptus, which was probably imported from Australia and grows for the greater part in the New Territories. During the summer months, from May until November, areas in Hong Kong that are farther removed from the concrete jungle can resemble a blossoming garden. Here one comes across various species of rhododendron shrubs as well as magnolia, hibiscus and oleander. Their blossoms turn the fields yellow, red, pink and white. More than 60 different species of orchids and white lilies, roses, irises, gardenias and camellias are encountered frequently. These flowers grow along the edges of fields and hillsides, sometimes also in small private gardens. The flowers sold on markets, however, are almost all imported from Taiwan or Japan by air-freight. For this reason, and because it is not common practice in Asia to decorate rooms with large bouquets, flowers are quite expensive.

The visitor can admire an exclusive collection of East Asian flowers, trees

Ailantus glandulosa

and shrubs at Hong Kong's Botanical Garden.

The most conspicuous members of Hong Kong's **animal world** are undoubtedly the many large to small and very colourful butterflies. Experts claim that they can hold their own in terms of variety and beauty against their more famous counterparts in Central and South America.

A number of songbirds are found here which also occur in Europe. Of these, the nightingale is especially beloved and revered by the Chinese. In rural regions and parks one will often see older men going for walks carrying birdcages with them. They stop to talk with other bird lovers, or simply relax and enjoy the singing of their feathered friends. About 300 species of Far Eastern birds can be admired at the aviary in the Botanical Garden. Eagles and buzzards frequent the rocky coastline of the New Territories.

There are also many different species of reptiles in Hong Kong.

Besides various harmless lizards and tiny geckos, a number of snake species have been registered, including venomous cobras, coral snakes and green bamboo snakes. (Even though one will rarely encounter any of these, it is still advisable to wear high-topped shoes or boots when hiking around more outlying areas.) There's a better chance of seeing apes, wild boars, porcupines and an occasional squirrel.

The waters surrounding Hong Kong are rich in species of fish, molluscs, corals and other marine life. The aquariums at Ocean Park, located on the southern shore of Hong Kong Island, provide the visitor with an excellent introduction to local saltwater and freshwater fauna.

(Jacobs)

The People

There really is no such thing as a "Hong Kongese", unless one chooses to apply the term in general to all of those either born or living in Hong Kong. Of the approximately 5.5 million inhabitants of the crown colony, only 22,000 (i. e. less than a half per cent) are British. Immigrants from other Commonwealth states include 8,000 East Indians, 5,000 Malaysians, 5,000 Australians and 2,500 Canadians. Furthermore, there are some 7,000 Americans and 1,500 Germans as well as smaller numbers of Portuguese, French, Dutch, Indonesians, Filipinos and Pakistanis. All together, the non-Chinese inhabitants barely make up two per cent of the population.

The Chinese population can also be statistically subdivided. According to the census of 1981, 41 per cent of the Chinese population listed territories outside Hong Kong as their place of origin. This means they are refugees from either the People's Republic of China or Taiwan, or they are here on official business for the People's Republic, Taiwan or Macau.

The Hoklo and Tanka, the boat people of Hong Kong's harbours, must have arrived several centuries ago. Exact dates are unknown. It is said that they were branded as traitors some 2,000 years ago and exiled to live on the sea. It wasn't until the 18th century that they were permitted to settle down again along the natural harbours. This story, however, may well belong to the realm of legends. Some social scientists believe that these people are not even of Chinese origin, but that they originally lived in Southeast Asia and then travelled in their boats to the southern coast of China by way of Malaysian territory. At any rate, they have always made a living as fishermen and coastal traders. Coastal trade was often prohibited by local rulers, so they became smugglers. About 30,000 of the 70,000 people living on board boats today still pursue their vocation on the sea. Others have regular jobs on land, but continue to live in their traditional floating homes. The true Han Chinese, who consider themselves superior to all other groups, view the boat people as second-class beings. It has become official policy to encourage them to move from the polluted harbours and dangerous junks to land areas.

Repeatedly over the centuries, various clans have settled on the mainland, in Kowloon and the New Territories. These people had usually fled across the mighty chain of hills and into the remotest corner of the empire for either political or economic reasons. The Hakka, a farming people from more northerly regions, began to arrive here in the 17th century. Prior to this they led a nomadic life, often changing their area of settlement. Their social structure is fairly unique. Literally translated, their name means "guest people". Women play the dominant role in this group, which is especially evident in the control they exercise over commercial activities, be it trading at the market or carrying bricks at construction sites in the New Territories. They are easy to recognize because they usually wear hats with wide brims and black veils. They also like to smoke small pipes that probably don't just *look* like opium pipes.

Thus the British found a varied but also sparse population when they decided to settle in this area in the middle of the 19th century. Immediately after colonization, whole families of Chinese moved to Hong Kong, primarily from the adjacent area of

what is now Guangdong Province. At first they came voluntarily, looking for work; later on, more and more felt forced to make the move for political and economic reasons. Furthermore, Hong Kong became the centre for emigrating Chinese from all over the land, which brought together people from the four counners of China and led to the establishment of a network of connections all over the world.

Shortly after the British takeover, Hong Kong only had a population of 5,500. At first this figure grew rapidly, reaching 25,000 within six years, and then slowing down again. Following the takeover of Kowloon in 1860, the numbers climbed once more. By the end of the nineteenth century the number of inhabitants had more than doubled, from 125,000 in 1865 to 254,000 in 1898. Of these, 240,000 were Chinese.

The chaos resulting from the fall of the Chinese empire drove more people towards the south, a process that was only interrupted by the advent of World War I. But, after 1920, the number of inhabitants began to rise anew, especially after the refugees from the armed conflict between the Warlords and the Kuomintang started to pour in.

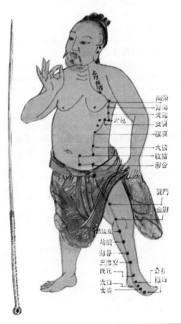

Instructional illustrations from an old Chinese medical text. Prospective physicians had to know the exact points on the body in which to insert the needles for acupuncture treatment. They were tested with a water-filled dummy; if the student found the correct spot, water would drip out.

By 1937, when the Japanese invaded China from the north, Hong Kong already had more than a million inhabitants. Four years later, as the Japanese stood before the gates of Hong Kong, this number had increased to 1,639,000. More than a million people were either killed or driven out by the Japanese. The end of World War II did not bring peace to the Far East: the 600,000 inhabitants left in Hong Kong after 1945 witnessed the influx of one and a half million refugees within the following five years. Another similar wave of immigrants began to arrive in the 1960's. By 1971 the number of people living in Hong Kong had passed the four million mark.

In the past, Hong Kong has always been open to refugees, regardless of whether they came from the People's Republic, Taiwan or Vietnam. But, the more crowded the city becomes, the closer the year 1997 approaches and the more the powers that be are willing and obliged to reach an agreement with Peking, the stricter the regulations governing the refugee problem become. Police squads patrol the borders of the New Territories and the shorelines. Refugees who are picked up are given a hot soup and sent back again whence they came. Regulations concerning identification have been tightened so that not everyone who has been able to find a member of the family in Hong Kong is automatically granted a permit of residence. Nevertheless, no one can say how many people manage to slip past the loose bamboo curtain each day and disappear into the city.

(Krücker)

Religions and Religious Thought

Wherever the Chinese come to control a city, their philosophy and religion eventually also rise to dominance. As far as East Asia is concerned, philosophy and religion flow together and it is difficult to differentiate between the two. This is due primarily to the fact that Asian religions tend neither to build churches nor to engage in aggressive missionary work, as is the case with Christianity or Islam. Religion is viewed here as a private agreement between an individual within a family and the gods. And the Chinese know a great many of the latter. It doesn't really matter whether they be of traditional or modern origin, just as long as they are effective. The more one supplicates, the better is the chance that one or the other will actually help.

Gods, too, are often pressed for time, or have gone off someplace, or are in a bad mood. Thus the daily religious practices of the Chinese are by nature eclectic and organized according to a pragmatic point of view.

The traditional philosophies/religions are Taoism and Confucianism. Then there is Buddhism, which originated in India but quickly spread to the whole of China.

Taoism is based on the teachings of Lao Zi (Lao-tse, literally "The Ancient One"). This is an honorary name – one which, according to legend, was given to an imperial civil servant of the 6th century who withdrew to the mountains in order to meditate. He is said to be the author of the 5,000-character *Dao De Jing* (Tao Te King). It is much more likely, however, that this collection of thoughts and popular sayings was recorded two to three centuries later by Taoist hermits. Following the unification of the empire, Taoist thought spread all over China, but it had to contend continually with Confucianism and Buddhism. Since Taoist philosophy does not strive for power, it never became a state religion like Confucianism.

The central concept in Taoism is the *Tao* (often translated inadequately as "Way", "Wisdom", "Truth" and such). It is the individual's view of himself and his life. Ideally, everything is in harmony: nature, humans, humans with nature. A person is following his Tao if he does not assume a position that is in contradiction to his own self and nature. This can best be achieved by "non-interference", which has often been interpreted as pure passivity and a norm for hermitic life. In fact, however, just what is meant with "natural" behaviour is open to interpretation as well. At any rate, in the course of history Taoists were very popular among the people because, wise and well-educated as they were, they often criticized rulers for their greed and unnatural lust for power.

The scholar and imperial advisor, K'ung Quiu, was born in 551 B.C. in Qufu (Shandong), where he also died at the age of 72. It was only later that he received the honorary title of K'ung Fu-tse (Master K'ung), which Jesuit missionaries Latinized to Confucius. Confucius first took up the task of bringing the ruling classes back onto the right path, but this proved to be futile. Giving up, he withdrew to his private school, where he soon acquired a small circle of devoted students. The latter then put together the classic work of Confucianism: the *Lunyu*.

Almost all of his teachings were oriented towards the past. The right path was to be reached by reintroducing the customs and ritual ceremonies of the early Zhou era (beginning in the 11th century B.C.). A strict social hierarchy was established: the subject had to obey the ruler, the son the father, the wife the husband and the younger the elder. Virtuous performance of one's duty was the highest principle. On the other hand, rulers had to provide for the well-being of their subjects, a notion that further stabilized the rigid social structure.

It wasn't until two hundred years after the death of the great master that his teachings were finally adopted as a doctrine of state. The rulers of the Han era viewed them as an ideal instrument with which to consolidate their power. It was on the basis of these teachings that the administrative system of loyal officials was established; this continues to dominate the Chinese form of government today. Confucius himself was declared a saint posthumously and Qufu, his home town, became a place of pilgrimage.

Ancestor worship and ritual ceremonies are the main Confucian contributions to religion. As far as social norms are concerned, it institutionalized hierarchical thinking and the low standing of women.

Gautama Siddhartha, the enlightened son of a noble, began to preach his way to attain bliss to people living all along the Ganges Valley some 500 years before the birth of Christ. Merchants and traders carried his teachings eastward and Buddhism soon rose to become the foremost religion in Asia. Even though the earliest proven Buddhist settlement in China dates back to 65 A.D., Buddhism was not able to gain a solid foothold there until 300 years later, following the heyday of Confucianism. It reached the first peak of its development in the 6th century, but this was terminated abruptly after 955 A.D. with the persecution of Buddhists all over the country. It did not regain its former position until the Ming era (1368–1644).

Buddhism agrees well with the Chinese way of thinking. It views humans as suffering beings who can, however, rid themselves of their woes and attain nirvana by following the right "path"; with a little assistance from the deities, of course. Nirvana is the overcoming of all differences, the perfect synthesis of opposites which is also strived for in Taoism. Like other Chinese religions, Buddhism sees the striving for happiness as a private matter, which every individual must confront and solve for himself. Those who don't help themselves cannot expect favours from the gods.

Other than the followers of the dominant East Asian religions outlined above, there are still some 400,000 members of various Christian denominations, 50,000 Moslems, 10,000 Hindus and about 1,000 Jews in Hong Kong.   (Krücker)

Ancestor Worship and Lucky Numbers

The colourful and loud procession with its clamouring crowds, its musicians and its bright red signs bordered with wreaths and multi-coloured flags moved at a halting, leisurely pace that seemed out of place in the hectic tempo of Kowloon. A funeral procession, as it turned out. Two men carried a three-storeyed house made of red papier-mâché. The interior was furnished with everything one could possibly desire: a large built-in kitchen with an electric stove, a dishwasher, refrigerator, deep-freeze and grill; two large and two small bedrooms with pompous furnishings; a living room complete with television, stereo and a mahjong table. The small annex was probably intended as living quarters for servants. Everything was done in miniature – may the deceased reside in such a palace in his next and better life!

Later on we had a look at the family altar in the temple. A photograph of the deceased stood there; beside it lay some rice, vegetables, meat and fish as provisions for the journey. There was even a half-pack of cigarettes as well as some self-printed money so that he could purchase his way into a better future.

It was a typical Chinese funeral ceremony. Regardless of which religious denomination one may belong to, superstitious beliefs still predominate among modern-day Hong Kong Chinese. Even baptized Christians still go to Taoist or Buddhist temples to have priests foretell their future with the help of a few wooden sticks or to have their palms read.

Prior to building a house people inevitably look up a *feng-shui* specialist and ask if the site is appropriate or whether it might be located on the tail or the head of a dragon, in which case no Chinese in his right mind would ever erect a building there. Jade amulets are worn as protection against all sorts of possible mishaps. And should something negative occur after all, then there is no doubt at all that a revengeful ghost of some deceased who was buried in the wrong place is to be held responsible.

Numbers play a very important role in matters of fortune and misfortune. Thirteen is considered to be an unlucky number in China, too, which is why most of the highrisers do not have a floor with that numeral – no one would dream of living there. Another unlucky number is four, because in its Cantonese pronunciation it can also mean "death". Lucky numbers are most effectively demonstrated in connection with that most cherished status symbol of the Hong Kong Chinese: the numberplates of luxury cars from England, Germany or the United States. It may even be that more is paid for the numberplate than for the rest of the car. A certain businessman, for instance, is known to have paid the equivalent of US$ 132,000 for the lucky number 3. It signifies "life and fertility". Other lucky numbers are 2: "everything will work out easily"; 6: "long life"; 8: "wealth"; and 9: "eternity". Then there is still the possibility of combining numbers, taking the sum of the digits or interpreting them in some other way to get a positive prediction. Fortune or misfortune ("joss") may depend upon the gods, but humans have to reach out and grasp the former.

(Jacobs)

Calendar of Festive Events

The Chinese love festive occasions and holidays, and they tend to celebrate with candid joy and a propensity for good food and drink. As public holidays are generally determined on the basis of the traditional Chinese moon calendar, the dates according to the official Gregorian calendar will vary slightly from year to year.

The cycle begins with the **Chinese New Year,** on the first three days of the first moon (January or February according to the Western calendar). It is both the most important and the lengthiest of Chinese festivities. Preparations begin two weeks prior to the actual New Year's Day, reaching an interim climax on the 23rd day of the twelfth moon of the old year, when the **Feast of the Kitchen God** is celebrated. On this day the kitchen god flies up to heaven to make a report to his master, the Jade Emperor, concerning his work down on earth. Of course, he is only supposed to have good things to say about each family, which is why he is offered tasty morsels and his mouth

smeared with honey (to sweeten his words). Once the kitchen god has been satisfied the cleaning-up activities commence, as well as shopping for presents and new clothes, preparing of New Year's pictures and sayings, and decorating of houses. All quarrelling must cease, unfinished business must be taken care of and all debts paid. The new year is supposed to be a new beginning in every sense of the word. Everybody has to get up early on New Year's Day, because all those who sleep late will be lazy for the rest of the year.

The Hong Kong Chinese also celebrate the Chinese New Year with traditional parades and tremendous fireworks displays. Festive meals can last from a few hours to several days (with interruptions, of course). Relatives or friends are visited and given brand-new bank notes as a symbol of fortune for the coming year. And, last but not least, a lot of gambling goes on, one of the favourite Chinese pastimes, and one which often thwarts the resolution to be free of all debts!

Quing Ming (Ching Ming) is a sort of commemorative day for the

whole year. Offerings are made to this god all over the waters surrounding Hong Kong, but the most impressive ceremonies take place in Bei Di's temple on the tiny island of Cheung Chau.

Tin Hau, "Heavenly Queen", is honoured every year on the 23rd day of the third moon. According to tradition, she lived in the 11th century and had the rare ability to predict storms, whereby she saved the lives of many fishermen and seamen. Many temples have been erected in her honour, especially in fishing villages along the shores of southern China as well as in Hong Kong and Macau. Her feast day is celebrated with lion dances.

The **Cheung Chau Bun Festival,** one of the most important Taoist celebrations, begins on the 8th day of the fourth moon and lasts for four days. Offerings are made on the island of Cheung Chau to placate the revengeful ghosts and restless souls of butchered animals. Especially worth seeing is the colourful procession that takes place on the last day of the festival.

deceased. It takes place each year on the 106th day after the beginning of winter, falling on or around April 5. On this day the inhabitants of Hong Kong and Macau will clean up the graves of their deceased relatives and bring them a few offerings. This event also concludes with a regular feast, only here the bill of fare is limited to cold dishes as it is forbidden to make fire for a period of three days.

On the third day of the third moon the birthday of **Bei Di** is celebrated. Bei Di is the "Spirit of the North" and God of the Sea, to whom seamen and fishermen entrust their lives for a

The **Bathing of Buddha** (Birthday of Lord Buddha), the most important Buddhist ceremony, is also celebrated in Hong Kong in honour of the birth of the Indian founder of this religion, Gautama Siddhartha. Celebrations here also begin on the 8th day of the fourth moon. The act of bathing all of the Buddha statues symbolically washes away all sins and opens the way for wisdom. This ceremony commemorates a mythological event: nine dragons are said to have sprayed water when Buddha was born.

The **Dragon Boat Festival** honours the poet Qu Yuan (Chu Yuan) and is also referred to as the "Day of the Poet". Qu Yuan apparently drowned himself in protest against a decadent and corrupt government more than two thousand years ago. Fishermen, who had observed the scene, raced their dragon-shaped boats in an effort to save the much-beloved poet. Arriving too late, they sprinkled rice where he went down so that the fish would feed on it rather than on his body. Feeding the fish and dragon boat racing have remained a tradition in southern China. The Dragon Boat Festival begins on the 5th day of the fifth moon (June or July) and is *the* highlight of Hong Kong's touristic year. The international dragon boat races taking place in Hong Kong at that time are viewed as an unofficial world championship. Rowing teams from the West (e. g. Oxford University) also participate in this event, albeit without much success!

Seven Sisters is a festive day devoted to young girls and lovers, taking place on the 7th day of the seventh moon. According to legend, the youngest of the emperor's seven daughters was an excellent weaver and her products were much cherished at the imperial court. When, following her marriage to a cowherd, she began to neglect her duties as a weaver, she was summoned back to court. From then on she was only allowed to see her husband once a year: on the 7th day of the seventh moon.

Both Buddhists and Taoists honour their ancestors during the **Hungry Ghosts Festival.** Buddhists also present their monks with baskets of fruit, victuals and other gifts in order to ensure that they will be especially thorough in their care of the ancestors' spirits. This festival takes place on the 14th day of the seventh moon.

The **Mid-Autumn Festival,** also called Moon Cake Festival, takes place on the 15th day of the eighth moon. It is dedicated to the observation of the moon, a tradition that goes back to the fourth century. The Chinese climb up hills and mountains – today they may also opt for the tops of highrisers – in order to get a good look at the earth's natural satellite. Children take along colourful lanterns. Moon cakes made of lotus seeds, nuts and sometimes also ground beans are handed out during the festival. A special treat at this time is the Lantern Carnival in Hong Kong's Victoria Park, which goes on for two days and attracts nearly half a million visitors each year.

The **Chung Yeung Festival** is a public holiday in Hong Kong, also referred to as "Mountaineer's Day" (9th day of the ninth month). The tradition to climb a mountain on this particular day is based on the story of Hung Qing, a man who had been warned by a prophesy that he would die on that day. Following the advice of his teacher, he climbed the highest mountain within reach and remained there until the next day. It is said that upon his return he found all of his cattle and domestic animals dead. But nothing had happened to him or his family. *(Jacobs)*

Museums

Hong Kong Museum of Art
10th and 11th Floor, City Hall, Connaught Road, Central
Open Mon., Tues., Wed. and Fri. from 10 a.m. to 6 p.m.; Sundays and public holidays from 1 p.m. to 6 p.m.

Chinese antiques from all dynasties; in particular, porcelain, paintings, calligraphy, ceramics, bronze, enamel, and jade works. Furthermore, prints, lithographs and oil paintings from the 18th and 19th centuries depicting the encounter between Europeans and Chinese. Regular exhibitions of contemporary artists.

Hong Kong Space Museum
Salisbury Road, Kowloon
Tues. from 7 p.m. to 10 p.m.; on all other days from 9 a.m. to 1 p.m., 2 p.m. to 6 p.m. and 7 p.m. to 10 p.m. Showings at the planetarium: Sun. and Thurs. 12 noon; Tues. and Fri. 6 p.m.; Wed. and Sat. 9 p.m. Simultaneous translations into several languages.

The showings include explanations of the firmament over Hong Kong and present a theory for the origin of the planet Earth. Exhibits include ancient Chinese astronomical instruments and drawings, rockets, satellites and astronaut suits.

Fung Ping Shan Museum
Hong Kong University, 94 Bonham Road, Hong Kong
Mon., Tues., Wed. and Fri. 10 a.m. to 6 p.m.

Bronze vessels from the Shang era (from about 16th to 11th century B.C.) and Zhou Dynasty (circa 11th century to 221 B.C.); ceramic sepulchral objects from the Han Dynasty (206 B.C. to 220 A.D.) and porcelain representative of the period from the Song Dynasty (960 to 1279 A.D.) to the Qing Dynasty (1644 to 1911). Also contains paintings and a collection of Buddha statues from India.

Hong Kong Museum of History
4th Floor, Star House, Nathan Road, Kowloon
Open daily except Friday from 10 a.m. to 6 p.m.; Sundays and public holidays 1 p.m. to 6 p.m.

Outline of Hong Kong's history with photographs and models; history of the fishing industry; nearly 5,000-year-old archaeological finds from the island of Lamma.

Lei Cheng Museum
Tonkin Street, Kowloon
Open daily except Thursday from 10 a.m. to 1 p.m. and 2 p.m. to 6 p.m.; Sundays and public holidays (except during Chinese New Year and Christmas) from 1 p.m. to 6 p.m.

A 2,000-year-old tomb (see Hong Kong from A to Z).

Art Gallery of the Chinese University
Institute of Chinese Studies, Shatin, New Territories.
Open Mon. to Sat. from 9.30 a.m. to 4.30 p.m.; on Sundays and public holidays from 12.30 p.m. to 5.30 p.m.

Exhibits by artists from neighbouring Guangdong Province dating from the era of the Ming Dynasty (1368–1644) to the present. Large collection of bronze stamps and seals from the Han and Qing eras.

Museum of Chinese Historical Relics

1st Floor, Causeway Centre
Harbour Road, Wanchai, Hong Kong
Open daily from 10 a.m. to 6 p.m.

Exhibitions of Chinese cultural treasures from certain dynasties or regions. Taped commentary in English.

Flagstaff House, Museum of Teaware

Victoria Barracks,
Cotton Tree Drive, Hong Kong
Open daily except Wed. from 10 a.m. to 5 p.m.

Located in one of the few original colonial buildings still standing. Contains a collection of teaware from the 7th century to the present.

Pao Sui Loong Galleries

Hong Kong Arts Centre,
Harbour Road, Wanchai, Hong Kong
Open daily from 10 a.m. to 8 p.m.

Regular exhibitions of works by contemporary Chinese artists from the People's Republic and Hong Kong.

Hong Kong Railway Museum

On Fu Road, Tai Po, New Territories

Exhibits from the early days of the railroad in Hong Kong.

Song Dynasty Village, Wax Museum

Lai Chi Kok, Kowloon

Wax figures of famous persons in Chinese history. Can only be visited in conjunction with a tour through the village (see Hong Kong from A to Z).

Shopping

No one has ever tried to count them all or list their names – the number of shops in Hong Kong is astronomical. Incomprehensible for most non-Asians is the fact that these shops continue to exist side by side, and that some even generate fortunes.

Feverish activity and speed may dictate the daily routine in this city, but there are two activities for which the Chinese take their time: eating and shopping. In Hong Kong one doesn't just simply go shopping.

Here, the act of purchasing becomes a sort of ritual, and bargaining is the essence of every transaction. Those who simply pay the price demanded without complaining will be penalized, and justly so in the eyes of the trader. The former can be certain that they have paid far too much for the product as a kind of compensation for having spoiled the trader's chance to practice his bargaining skills.

Hong Kong prides itself – and justly so – on being one of the best-value shopping areas of the world. The British Crown Colony happens to be a free port. Nearly every possible kind of product may be imported without duty having to be paid. Supply and demand dictate the prices, and the low wages. Excessive supply and stiff competition result primarily in an advantage for those who plan to do some shopping. Indeed, for many visitors the primary objective of their trip seems to be just that. Official statistics show that tourists end up leaving 60% of their travel funds at the shops in Hong Kong. They spend their money at the jeweller's or optician's, in camera shops, at the watch dealer's, at shops selling porcelain and glass products, furniture, carpets, fashions, shoes and leather goods, or at one of the better known tailor's businesses in town.

Speaking about tailors: you can still get a custom-made suit in Hong Kong for a reasonable price, about the same as you would pay for a ready-made one in Europe. But forget the 24-hour suit. Even the good, creative and fast Hong Kong tailors need at least three days and one fitting to produce a suit that fits well.

The choice of where to go to spend that holiday money is entirely up to the individual. Tsimshatsui is noted both for its shops along the Nathan Road and for its shopping centres such as the New World Centre, Harbour City Complex and Ocean Terminal; then there's the Central District on the Hong Kong side, as well as the Causeway Bay area. But, wherever you decide to go,

a few tips before you set off on your shopping spree.

Often, the prices on tags or the sums first demanded can be bargained down by about 30 to 40 per cent. Recently, however, this applies more and more to smaller shops only. Haggling is totally out of the question in department stores belonging to companies based in the People's Republic of China.

Always ask for a detailed bill of sale. If you purchase watches, cameras or electronic equipment be sure a worldwide guarantee from the producer is included. In the case of jewellery, check that the bill of sale lists exactly the weight, carat and

proportion of gold or silver in a particular piece.

The best insurance for visitors is to do their shopping at stores affiliated with the Hong Kong Tourist Association (HKTA): these can easily be recognized by stickers bearing an image of a black junk on doors or shop windows. Should you, upon your return home, detect something amiss with the goods you purchased, the HKTA will arrange for the dealer to either refund your money or replace the faulty product. The HKTA also provides visitors with an official shopping guide, "Best of Hong Kong Shopping", which is a great help, especially considering the great number of shops available.

Let us assume, for instance, you are interested in jewellery. Here there are more than 1,100 official dealers selling about US$ 1.5 billion worth of jewellery each year. Hong Kong is the third largest gold-trading centre of the world; as a diamond-cutting centre it ranks fifth in the world and as export centre for jewellery, a proud third. Prices on average are about 20 to 30% lower than in Europe. Other than enough cash, a prospective buyer should bring two things with him/her: a concrete notion of what he/she wants to buy, and ample time to compare prices and quality in the various stores.

Usually the dealer will also take his time. To a cup of Chinese tea, a cool beer or ice-cold Coke, he will present his selection of rings or necklaces, commenting on the quality of each piece and, above all, explaining why it is well worth the "absolutely lowest" price quoted … only to lower it again somewhat later. Gold, silver or platinum will be sold by the gramme; gems are valued according to carat, colour, purity and cut. The value of pearls will depend upon size, colour and perfection of their smooth, rounded surface – preferably all should be matched individually. Jade is judged by intensity and uniformity of colour, a slight translucence and a proper feel – here the layman will have to depend entirely upon the evaluation of the dealer.

Those who are not necessarily looking for top-quality jade can enjoy shopping at the jade street markets along Canton Road (Kowloon). The selection is ample indeed: thousands of pieces of jewellery and carvings are available to choose from, at very reasonable prices.

The supply of watches, cameras, optical goods and electronic gadgets is equally enormous. Here you will find every brand made in the world and prices will be 20% lower than they are in Europe. Again, compare prices and stores, demand manufacturers' guarantees, and remove products from their packages to check them and compare the serial numbers with those on the guarantee.

Nowhere else outside of the People's Republic are Chinese handicrafts, antiques, furniture and, above all, the famous Chinese rugs offered in such quantities and at such low prices as in Hong Kong. Shipping products home is no problem either: every dealer will be familiar with the best shipping rates and quickest freight connections.   (Jacobs)

Nightlife

The world of Suzie Wong is a thing of the past. Nevertheless, the neon signs still burn in Wanchai and in the side streets leading off Nathan Road in Kowloon. Bright, gaudy and obtrusive, they advertize bars and nightclubs with equally gaudy and obtrusive hostesses. Most of them are tourist traps, catering primarily to Japanese visitors. A few have already adopted Japanese names. A German press correspondent once aptly described the nightclubs with the words "cheap and expensive". Cheap, as far as standards are concerned, and expensive in terms of drinks.

Perhaps the following suggestions may be of help to anyone who should happen to land in one of these establishments. Always pay immediately for each drink. This will avoid likely discussions concerning the bill at a later hour. If a hostess asks for a drink (which will usually happen within two minutes at the very most), then remind her most cordially that a glass of tea cannot cost more than HK$ 25 and politely deny her request.

Those who are not that adventurous as far as bars, nightclubs and discotheques are concerned should stick to the entertainment facilities at hotels. Quite popular spots on Hong Kong Island include the "Captain's Bar" in the Mandarin Hotel, the "Den" in the Hilton and the "Dickens Bar" in the Excelsior; the places to go to in Kowloon are the "Polaris" on the top floor of the Hyatt Regency Hotel and "Another World" in the Holiday Inn Golden Mile. "Bar City" in the basement of the New World Shopping Centre has no less than seven bars and nightclubs and is well worth a visit. Practically an institution and perfectly harmless for even the most inexperienced tourist, "Bottoms Up" on Hankow Road, close to the Hyatt Hotel, is frequented by successful Hong Kong businessmen and "officials" – often with their wives – as well as by travellers from all over the world; clientele spend their time in conversation with each other or with one of the topless waitresses serving at any of the five lively round bars.

But then there is more to nightlife in Hong Kong than just bars and nightclubs: evenings certainly never need be boring. For instance, there are the Chinese theatre-restaurants, such as the one in the Miramar Hotel in Kowloon or "Pearl City" on the Island. Here a visitor can enjoy Chinese operas, music, dances and puppet shows while savouring a (quite recommendable) Cantonese meal.

Another option would be an evening spent cruising the harbour; this comes complete with dinner to the accompaniment of music and a spectacular view of Hong Kong and Kowloon by night.

Concerts by the internationally renowned Hong Kong Philharmonic and other visiting orchestras take place quite frequently. Or you could just go for an evening stroll along Temple Street or "Poor Man's Night-club" on the parking lots next to the Macau-Ferry docks in Hong Kong. Victoria Peak offers a breathtaking view of harbour and city. There are theatre performances and readings of literary works, while about one hundred cinemas show films from all over the world (mostly in English with Chinese subtitles). If you happen to have been out sightseeing during the day, then you could even spend the evening shopping as many stores stay open until 10 or 11 p.m.

(Jacobs)

Sports in Hong Kong

Horse-Racing: Favourite spectator sport among Chinese and English-men, who are crazy about betting. There are two tracks: the famous, tra-ditional one in Happy Valley on the Island and a new, modern one in Shatin, New Territories. During the season (September until May), races take place on most Saturday after-noons, on many Wednesday evenings and on a few Sunday afternoons.

Riding: If you prefer to be on the back of a horse yourself, there are three riding schools to choose from (all hire out horses by the hour): Shatin Riding School in the New Ter-ritories, Hong Kong Riding Academy on the Island, and the school in the vicinity of the Po Lin Monastery on the island of Lantau.

Golf: The Royal Hong Kong Golf Club in Fanling (New Territories) has three 18-hole courses. It is open to guests on weekdays and the green fee of HK$ 480 per day includes use of club facilities such as swimming pool, sauna, bars and restaurants.

The club also has a 9-hole course at Deep Water Bay – green fees are HK$ 100. There is yet another golf course at Shek 0.

Tennis: Those who always carry a racket with them will find enough courts in Hong Kong; these are, how-ever, quite well frequented. Public courts are available at Victoria Park (Causeway Bay), on Bowen Road, in the tennis centre on Wongneichung Gap Road on the Island, as well as in Kowloon's Tsai Park. A number of hotels have courts for the use of guests only.

The Hong Kong annual classic (Open Championship) takes place each November. Tickets to the event can be arranged through Hong Kong Tennis Patrons' Association Ltd., Room 406, 4/F, 48–51 Chatham Road, Kowloon.

Squash: Courts can be rented at the Queen Elizabeth Stadium, Victoria Park and Kowloon's Tsai Park, daily from 7 a.m. to 11 p.m. Furthermore, there are a number of private clubs where one can become a temporary member.

Table Tennis: A popular sport all over East Asia. Public facilities are available for a low rental fee at Morse Park, Cheung Sha Wan and in Boundary Street.

Bowling: This evening sport has been experiencing a veritable boom in Hong Kong in recent years. More and more bowling alleys are being constructed, so you should have little trouble finding one. In Kowloon, for instance, there is the Brunswick Centre on Middle Road; on the Island there is the Four Seas Bowling Centre, City Plaza, Taikoo Shing. Facilities are open practically round the clock.

Ice-skating: The largest ice-skating rink in all of Southeast Asia is located at Laichikok Amusement Park (open daily from 11 a.m. to 10.15 p.m.). Ice-skating classes are available at the City Plaza rink, Taikoo Shing.

Sailing: There are ten major sailing associations in Hong Kong. Nevertheless, chartering a yacht is difficult and expensive. Inquire at the Royal Yacht Club. A few of the junks moored at the Boating Centre can be hired for pleasure tours. Numerous smaller sailing crafts are available at the Silvermine Bay Beach Hotel on Lantau Island.

Surfing: Possible at several beaches. Inquire at the Windsurfing Associa-

tion of Hong Kong, G. P. O. Box 10833, Hong Kong.

Water-Skiing: Most of the public beaches are not open to water-skiers. The best possibilities are at the southernmost beaches of Hong Kong Island, such as Deep Water Bay, where boats and skis are available for hire.

Scuba Diving: Divers can get in touch with the Sea Dragon Skin Divers Club, which organizes diving expeditions on weekends to offshore islands. Information available from Hong Kong Underwater Federation, G.P.O. Box 9012, Hong Kong.

Swimming: You have a choice between a total of 40 public beaches in the New Territories, on Hong Kong Island and on offshore islands. During summer weekends the beaches are often overcrowded. The most popular beaches are located in the southern part of Hong Kong: Repulse Bay, Deep Water Bay, Middle Bay, Chung Hom Kok and Stanley. Other beaches: Shek O and Big Wave in the southeast; Clear Water Bay, Silverstrand Beach, Camper's Beach, Trio Beach and Sharp Island in the eastern part of the New Territories; Silvermine Bay, Cheung Sha and Discovery Bay on Lantau Island; and Picnic Bay and Cheung Chan on Lamma Island.

The sports centres at Victoria Park and Kowloon's Tsai Park have swimming pools. Numerous hotels have their own pools, which are often open to non-resident guests.

Kung Fu: Those interested in this East Asian form of martial art should contact the Chinese Martial Arts Association, 687 Nathan Road, 8th Floor, Kowloon.

Sports Arenas: A number of East and/or Southeast Asian sports events take place in Hong Kong. Check with the local press or the Hong Kong Tourist Association for dates. Several large sports arenas or stadiums are open to the public.

Besides theatre performances and exhibitions, the Hong Kong Coliseum (seating capacity 12,500) is the venue of basketball and volleyball games. In Shatin (New Territories) there is the Jubilee Sports Centre with a wide range of indoor and outdoor facilities. The Queen Elizabeth Stadium (seating capacity 3,500) opened in 1980; here there are facilities for basketball, volleyball, badminton, squash and table tennis. It is located in Wanchai, Hong Kong Island.

(Jacobs/Krücker)

Media

All aerials in the surroundings, even those in the southern part of the People's Republic, are turned towards Hong Kong. This city is one of the major media centres of Southeast Asia, especially as far as printed media is concerned.

Of the approximately 120 newspapers appearing in Hong Kong, more than 100 are Chinese and the remainder English. Many of the Chinese papers are printed on a single page that can be folded into four and thus handily folded by the reader at any time for a quick glance at a particular section. Many Chinese will purchase a fresh newspaper every morning, afternoon and evening.

The choice of English-language papers is more limited. The *South China Morning Post* and *Hong Kong Standard* appear daily. In addition, editions of international papers like the *International Herald Tribune* and *Asian Wall Street Journal* are printed locally. The *Star* is a tabloid containing the latest gossip.

Other than at regular stores, these newspapers and magazines are sold by paperboys who roam the already overcrowded streets in the early morning and late in the afternoon. Thus one can obtain a paper hot off the press at all major intersections and along busy business streets.

Foreign papers and magazines are available primarily at larger newspaper stands and international hotels. Due to shipping, however, they tend to be quite expensive.

Colour television is practically a standard feature in every middle class hotel and upwards. There are two private stations in Hong Kong: *Asia Television (ATV)* and *Television Broadcasts (TVB)* with two channels each, one in Cantonese and the other in English. Films will usually have subtitles in the other language;

foreign films occasionally have subtitles in both Cantonese and English. Frequent commercial breaks (advertising is often quite entertaining) draw out films for hours.

Two channels broadcast almost round the clock while the other two start early afternoon and remain on the air until after midnight. Television programmes are printed up in local newspapers.

Three radio stations operating nine channels provide the city with music and information 24 hours a day. *Radio Television Hong Kong (RTHK)*, which is subsidized by the government, operates two Cantonese channels, two English ones, and another that is bilingual. This station is also tied to the *BBC World Service*. The privately-operated *Commercial Radio*, which gets its funds from commercials (as the name implies), broadcasts on two Cantonese and one English channel. Then there is still the channel operated by the *British Forces Broadcasting Service (BFBS)*. All three stations have brief newscasts every half hour.

Radio programmes are also printed in English-language papers. Listening to the radio, however, is not as popular in Hong Kong as watching television. Chances are that any music you might hear, be it pop or classic, will be blaring from cassette recorders rather than radios.

(Krücker)

Hong Kong from A to Z

The letter and number in parenthesis behind every place name indicates its location on the map on pp. 134 and 135, as well as on the foldout map at the back of the guide.

Aberdeen (E9) was formerly a fishing village and pirates' hideout, its reputation as such dating back to the 13th century. Even today the Chinese still refer to it as "Heung Keung Tsai" (Small Fragrant Harbour) rather than using the official name honouring a colonial minister. About 20,000 people live here in junks moored in the harbour.

A tour of the harbour on a sampan will take between 20 minutes and half an hour. Agree on a price before departure. Also worthwhile because of their interesting atmosphere and good food are the "floating restaurants".

On land, along Main Street, one can still find a few shops that may not yet have abandoned the old smuggler traditions entirely. Fisherman's Hall is the place where weddings and elections take place. Tin Hau Temple, dating back to 1851, becomes the focus of everyone's interest in April, on the day of festivities held in honour of its patron goddess. Excursions possible to Ap Lei Chau.

Amah Rock (C10), a hill located along the road from Shatin to Kowloon, can be seen from the Monastery of 10,000 Buddhas in Shatin. The Rock resembles a woman carrying a baby on her back. According to legend, it represtens a woman who, when her fisherman husband once failed to return from a voyage, waited day after day for his return. Finally, after a year had gone by, the gods took pity on the unfortunate wife and turned her into a rock.

Ap Lei Chau (E9), a small island just off Aberdeen, settled by boatbuilders.

Ferries, yachts, sailing boats and racing craft are made here, as well as traditional junks and sampans. Guided tours in English are available. This island, the name of which translates as "Duck Tongue Island", can be reached by way of a causeway.

Aw Boon Haw Gardens (Tiger Balm Gardens) (E10), a sort of Chinese Disneyland with candy-coloured, lighted bridges, pagodas, and statues representing gods or mythical beings. Certainly not to everyone's taste.

Mr. Aw Boon Haw made a fortune selling Tiger balm, a mentholated salve said to help with all sorts of ailments, especially headaches and colds. He had the park constructed in 1935 for about four million US-Dollars. His mausoleum and mansion are also located on the grounds. The latter contains a valuable jade collection which, however, can only be seen with a special permit obtainable from the Hong Kong Tourist Association.

Botanical Garden (D9), on Garden Road, Hong Kong Central. A shady, 7-hectare (17-acre) nature-oasis along the slope of the Peak. Here subtropical vegetation is combined with Chinese garden landscaping. The Chinese like to use this place early in the mornings to do their exercises in taijiquan (or tai chi chuan, shadow-boxing). There is also a small aviary holding about 700 birds representing some 300 different species. It can best be reached with the Peak Tram from stops on Macdonnell Road and Kennedy Road. The governor's palace is nearby.

Bride's Pool (A10), protected landscape in the northeastern part of the New Territories with many cascades and waterfalls. A popular spot for weekend picnics. The story behind its name is a sad one: many years ago a young bride was being carried in a sedan chair from her home village to that of her prospective husband. It was raining heavily when the party reached the pool and, as they were crossing the stream above it, one of the bearers slipped. The entire party plunged into the waters down below and was never seen again.

Castle Peak (C7) dominates the satellite city of Tuen Mun in the western part of the New Territories, the population of which is soon to reach the half-million mark. From the 583-metre (1,913 feet) summit of the Peak, one has a grand view (when the weather is clear) of the surrounding mountains, Deep Bay in the north, and the island of Lantau in the south. The Peak was also the former destination of the first road to open up the New Territories, Castle Peak Road, which was finished in 1919. In contrast to the modern expressway, it still leads through many small fishing villages. The valleys in this area are used agriculturally. There are interesting temples, e. g. Ching Chung Koon.

Causeway Bay (D10), located on the northern coast of Hong Kong Island, is hardly recognizable as a bay any more due to massive land reclamation projects. One hundred years ago it was an idyllic little place just out of town. Dinner on one of the sampans moored at Causeway Bay Typhoon Shelter is an interesting experience.

Following the construction of the Cross Harbour Tunnel, Causeway Bay developed into a modern sector with de luxe hotels, restaurants and nightclubs. Early in the mornings in Victoria Park one can see numerous, usually elderly, people practising taijiquan. Queen's College, oldest Anglo-Chinese school founded in 1862, is located on Tunglowan Road. Remnants from the days of opium dealers found in the older sector are Jardine's Bazar and Jardine's Crescent.

William Jardine was one of the first and most powerful of the opium traders who were responsible for the rise of Hong Kong in the 1840's.

Central District (D9), formerly called Queen's Town and later named Victoria, is located at the foot of Victoria Peak. It is the site of the first major settlement on Hong Kong Island. Unfortunately, most of the old colonial buildings have been torn down and replaced by administrative and office buildings as well as by skyscrapers belonging to banking establishments. The only colonial buildings to have survived are Flagstaff House (now a museum), Victoria and Murray Barracks (former quarters of the British Army, which the first governors had already wanted transferred out of town) and St. John's Cathedral (built 1849). The lower station of the Peak Tram is located close by. The greater part of this city sector is constructed on reclaimed land. The Star Ferry to Kowloon and other ferries to the New Territories depart from piers along the harbour here. Central District is certainly the most exclusive part of the island, at least as far as shop and business addresses are concerned. Administrative buildings are situated here along with numerous large banks, department stores and hotels.

Cheung Chau (E7/8), a barbell-shaped island east of Lantau, probably owes its name to the notorious pirate Cheung Po Tsai. The island can be reached from Hong Kong in an hour's journey by ferry. Cars are not allowed on the island, which ensures a certain degree of peace and quiet. The inhabitants of the town, located on the narrowest strip of the island, exude an air of South-Sea-Island serenity. They make a living fishing, farming and handicrafting. Evenings along the harbour get quite lively. The food served by numerous stands by the pier is simple but quite delicious.

There are a number of beaches situated here: Tung Wan, at the eastern part of town, is the largest and has the best facilities, but is certainly not the nicest. The water at Sai Wan is much cleaner. Visitors have a choice between three hotels.

Pak Tai Temple, built by Taoists in 1783, is well worth a visit. The principal deity honoured here, Pak Tai or "Spirit of the North", is said to have saved the inhabitants from an epidemic at one time. His image is flanked by two war gods, Thousand-Li Eye and Favourable Wind Ear. The temple also houses a 1.5-metre-(5 ft) long sword from the Song Dynasty (960–1279 A.D.). Made of iron, with a copper handle shaped like a dragon, the sword is shown to visitors upon request. All of the islanders gather here for a week each year in April or May to celebrate the famous Bun Festival.

Chinese University (B10), second university in Hong Kong, was founded in 1963 in the New Territories. Of special interest here is the art gallery, which features a survey of Chinese art from the Ming era (1368–1644) to the present. It is open daily (except Sundays) from 12.30 pm until 5.30 pm. The university has its own train station.

Ching Chung Koon (C7, built in 1959, comprises a Taoist temple with a home for the aged and vegetarian restaurant. A wide, stone stairway leads through a Chinese garden with numerous bonsai (dwarfed trees) to the main hall, which serves as a place of ancestor worship. The statues depicting two virgins are said to have been sculptured in Peking 300 years ago. The walls are decorated with paintings of famous Chinese generals; one of them specialized in killing dragons, while another subdued tigers. Small portraits of deceased persons line the walls of the ancestral hall. The library in this temple dedicated to one of Taoism's eight immortals contains more than 4,000 volumes of Taoist writings as well as numerous art treasures, such as a 200-year old lantern and a thousand-year-old jade seal.

Directly opposite the Ching Chung Koon Temple, two great 20-metre (60-foot) dragons confront visitors at the entrance to **Miu Fat Monastery.**

Miu Fat covers an area of 20,500 square metres (220,660 square feet) and is dominated by a main temple with thousands of buddha statues. The walls are decorated with Chinese and Thai paintings.

Clearwater Bay (D11), a bathing resort offering numerous leisure and sports activities (golf, tennis, badminton, squash) and quiet places for walks.

Once a year Tin Hau Temple on Joss House Bay becomes the destination of hundreds of decorated junks and sampans. Fishermen and pilgrims then celebrate the birthday of the goddess with processions, orchestras and lion dances. The present temple dates back to the 13th century and was built over the remains of one that was destroyed by a typhoon in the 11th century.

Close by is the prop-city of the Shaw brothers – Hong Kong's version of Hollywood – where many kung fu "Easterns" are produced.

Deepwater Bay (E9/10), one of Hong Kong's most popular beaches, located on the south side of Hong Kong Island. Fresh water showers, changing cubicles, washrooms and beverage stands are available to visitors here. The Hong Kong Country Club and Royal Hong Kong Golf Club further accentuate the exclusivity of this sector, in which numerous millionaires have erected their villas.

Fanling (B9) is considered to be one of the most beautiful traditional Chinese market towns in all of the New Territories; this is particularly true of the old section of town. Of special interest is Luen Wo Market, which has been a tradition since 1948. The town was founded by the Pang Clan about 600 years ago and today approximately 3,000 Chinese with that surname live here.

Happy Valley (E9/10), Hong Kong Island, where the first settlers who arrived in 1841 found malaria rather than happiness. The horse racing track remained after the settlers left, however, and for nine months of the year (September to May) it attracts large crowds of betters. Of further interest here are the five cemeteries – one each for Moslems, Catholics, Protestants, Parsees and Jews – lying due east of Queen's Road. Just behind the racecourse is Aw Boon Haw Gardens, formerly called Tiger Balm Gardens.

Kam Tin (B8), New Territories. The walled villages of Kam Tin date back to the end of the 13th century, when the Tang Clan provided the last emperor of the Song Dynasty (960–1279) refuge from his persecutors. The walls themselves were only built about 200 years ago, in response to increased attacks by pirates. They also repulsed the first onslaught of British soldiers in 1899, when these wanted to take over the New Territories. The wrought-iron gate was supposedly shipped to the British Isles then and remained there until 1925, when it was brought back to Hong Kong from Ireland.

Today, the inhabitants re-enact all aspects of China's feudal age for tourists, from the proper apparel to the art of calligraphy. Photographing allowed for cash only.

Lai Chi Kok (D9), a typical Chinese amusement park situated on the periphery of Kowloon, has betting games, cinemas, lotteries, acrobats, entertainers, a small zoo and an ice skating rink. Chinese operas and dances are performed in the evenings. Take bus line 6 A, which departs from the quay of the Star Ferry; opening hours are from 11 a.m. to 11 p.m. The park is located next to a village from the Song Dynasty.

Lamma (E/F 8/9), a mountainous and relatively unfrequented island, which can be reached in a 40-minute journey from Hong Kong. Construction workers unearthed numerous pottery shards, stone tools and bronze artifacts here, which indicate a very early settlement. Two fishing villages can be visited: Yung Shue Wan in the north and Sok Kwu Wan in the east. The latter can also be reached from Aberdeen; excellent fish restaurants along the quay. At weekends, however, a great number

of private boats crowd the bay. Those seeking peace and quiet then can take to the rocky trails around Mount Stenhouse (353 metres/1,158 feet) or along the nearly abandoned bays on the southern part of the island.

Lantau (D/E 5/8), largest island of the area, twice the size of Hong Kong Island. There are ferry links to Mui Wo on Silvermine Bay, as well as to Tai O on the western coast (only on Sundays and public holidays). A bus line operates between these two places.

The island is scenically wild and beautiful. Only about 30,000 people live on it – no wonder, then, that monks have sought seclusion here. The primary activity of visitors to this island will consist of hikes to the hills and mountains, of which Lantau Peak is the highest with 934 metres (3,064 feet). There are a number of places worth seeing on the way.

Silvermine Bay (Mui Wo) is the largest settlement on the island; its beaches and beach hotel provide a good touristic infrastructure. An abandoned mine in the Mui Wo valley gave the bay and town its name. There is another beach resort on **Discovery Bay** farther north.

A bus leaves from Silvermine Bay to the Buddhist **Po Lin Monastery,** which is situated on the plateau of Ngong Ping at an elevation of 750 metres (2,460 feet). The original temple was constructed in 1921; since then a pair of two-storeyed temples have been added to the complex. For a small fee visitors can try out a monk's life, sleeping on hard boards and eating only vegetarian food.

An ideal place for an afternoon tea or longer sojourn is **Lantau Tea Gardens,** Hong Kong's own tea plantation (not far from Po Lin), complete with camping facilities, bungalows and horses for hire.

The area around **Tung Chung** was the former refuge of the notorious pirate, Cheung Po Tsai, who was finally defeated by a Chinese-Portuguese fleet. Following this event, the Qing administration built a fort on the site and garrisoned imperial troops there to protect the area. Some of the cannons standing in the restored fort date back to the beginning of the 19th century.

There is a more peaceful atmosphere at the **Trappist monastery** near Tai Shui Hang, not least because the monks there have taken a vow of silence. The best way to reach the monastery is from Peng Chau Island, where the boats belonging to the order often land, or where one can hire a sampan for the passage. The monks have specialized in the production of dairy produce, which they deliver to a number of luxury hotels in Hong Kong. Simple overnight accommodation is available on reservation.

The small town of **Tai O** has been the centre of the salt panning industry in Hong Kong for more than one hundred years. Tanka people live here in their boats or stilt houses. A ferry provides passage to the small island on which the greater part of the town is situated. Numerous shops here offer handicraft products for sale.

Lei Cheng Uk's Tomb (D9) is located on Tonkin Street, Kowloon, and can be reached from the Star Ferry quay with bus line No. 2. The tomb, which was unearthed during construction work in 1955, dates back to the era of the Han Dynasty (206 B. C.–220 A. D.). This is indicated by the form of the vault and inscriptions. The tomb is made up of four chambers laid out in the form of a cross. Pottery and bronze artefacts had been placed in them, but neither a coffin nor a body were found. Archaeologists thus assume that it was either a tomb of honour or an empty tomb commemorating some ancestors who had passed away previously.

Lion Rock (D10), rock in the form of a lion's head. Lion Rock Country Park is one of the largest and most beautiful nature parks of the area. Situated in the New Territories.

Man Mo Temple (E9), built around 1848, is the oldest temple of the new settlement on Hong Kong's northern coast. This Taoist temple, situated on the corner of Hollywood Road and Ladder Street, is visited daily by a great number of believers. Consequently, there is always incense burning on large spiral coils hanging from the ceiling (some of these coils are several feet in diameter). The name of the temple is a typical example of Taoist synthesis of opposites: *man* means civilian and *mo* for its part, military. Man is the god of literates and government officials, and is supposed to have taught during the Tang era (618–907 A. D.). Guang Yu, the warlord, lived during the period of the Three Kingdoms (220–280).

Eight immortals guard the temple. The two solid brass stags inside symbolize longevity. On display are three sedan chairs that were once used to transport the sacred images through the town. The large bell was cast in 1846, the smaller one in 1897.

New Kowloon (D9/10) designates the adjoining section of Kowloon extending into the New Territories (leased from China). This extension was needed for large-scale housing projects, industrial complexes and factories.

Noon Day Gun (D10), a cannon standing on Causeway Bay, belongs to Jardine Matheson & Co. and fires a salute each day at 12 noon. This tradition goes back to the early colonial days, but its precise origin remains unknown. It is said that the cannon was fired in honour of the trading house's tai-pans or as a salute to incoming opium ships. In time, the administration prohibited the continuous racket, allowing only one round to be fired each day at noon. The directors of the enterprise also discharge the cannon (made in 1901) during New Year's Eve celebrations.

Ocean Park (E9), the largest oceanarium of the world. This huge marine amusement park (68 hectares/168 acres) was constructed in 1977 for the sum of 150 million HK-Dollars. The site is made up of two sections connected by a cable car. At the entrance one arrives at the botanical garden, complete with waterfalls, pools with freshwater fish, carousels, a zoo where children can pat the animals, and a huge aviary. Following a six-minute ride on the cable car, visitors arrive at the "Headland" where the more interesting events take place. Here an artificial atoll has been set up with beautiful coral reefs and over 300 species of marine animals, including numerous sharks, all of which can be observed through glass plates. Sea elephants, seals, sea lions and penguins swim about in a large basin complete with wave movement; conditions are geared to the natural environment of the animals. Porpoises and killer whales perform their tricks in "Ocean Theatre", the world's largest artificial basin; the arena has a seating capactiy of 4,000. From Ocean Park one has a grand view of Aberdeen, Deepwater Bay and Repulse Bay. On Sundays this mammoth creation of the Hong Kong leisure industry is often overcrowded. On Sundays, bus line No. 71 A takes visitors directly to the park from Central District. On weekdays, one has to take bus line 4 to Wah Fu and then transfer to line 73 (Aberdeen) or 48 (Wong Chuk Hang).

Adjoining Ocean Park is **Water World** (opened in 1984), a marine amusement park with swimming pools, slides, artificial beaches and a bight with wave movement. An additional entrance fee is charged.

Peng Chau (D8), a small island off Lantau, can be reached by ferry from Hong Kong Island. Starting point for a visit to Lantau's Trappist monastery. Motorized vehicles are not allowed on the island, making it a perfect place to enjoy the romantic atmosphere of Chinese fishing communities. Nevertheless, modern times are also in evidence: toys for the European market are produced here in outwork. One can also observe potters and artists at work in their shops.

The Temple of Tin Hau dates back to 1792 and contains a three-metre (10-foot) long shark's bone said to be 200 years old; it is venerated by fishermen.

Plover Cove Reservoir (B10/11). This huge reservoir ensures supplies of drinking water and well exemplifies the ingenuity and technical know-how of Hong Kong's inhabitants. Following a drought in 1966, great masses of earth and stone were dumped into the sea along the north-eastern shore of the New Territories, forming tremendous dams. Then the salt water was pumped out and the remaining basin refilled with fresh water brought in from the People's Republic via pipelines.

Possession Street (E9), presently situated at the centre of Victoria's Western District, marks the site where Commodore Sir J. J. Gordon Bremer took possession of the island for the British Crown on January 26, 1841, and raised the Union Jack. At that time, Queen's Road was the promenade running along the shore; the area between Queen's Road and the contemporary shoreline was reclaimed from the sea. Possession Street is closed off to motor traffic and thus preserves some of its original ambience.

Po Toi (F10/11) is one of the southernmost and smallest of the leased islands. Of special interest here is Ghost Rock: it bears enigmatic inscriptions, the origins of which are still subject to much discussion among historians. Some consider the inscribed symbols as proof of early settlement by the Khmer, while others hold them to be evidence of a visit by Arabian seafarers.

Visitors might also have a look at Po Toi's "ghost towns", settlements abandoned by their inhabitants in favour of Hong Kong and its presumed higher living standards. Those who have the time to do so should visit Po Toi on weekdays, crossing to the island on one of the small water taxis – at weekends and on public holidays the islet is entirely overrun.

Repulse Bay (E10), one of the most popular and populated beaches, is situated in the southern part of Hong Kong Island. Visitors will find all kinds of facilities here, including washrooms, restaurants, bars, kiosks and boat rentals.

Graham Greene used to write his novels on the terrace of the renowned Repulse Bay Hotel, where the world's great personalities were wont to sip their cocktails.

The bay received its name from the British war ship *Repulse,* which was employed against pirates during the early stages of colonization. The two statues standing before the Life Guard Club represent Tin Hau, protectress of fishermen and swimmers, and Kwun Yam, a goddess of mercy.

Sai Kung Peninsula (C11), one of the most beautiful and unspoilt areas in Hong Kong, is located in the southeastern part of the New Territories. Here one can go for pleasant walks along wooded hillsides. Boats can be rented in Hebe Haven; Sai Kung itself is a lively market town and fishing port.

Shatin (C10), a town in the New Territories with a number of interesting sights. Can easily be reached by train.

The **Monastery of 10,000 Buddhas** – there may well be some 12,800 of them – lies in the vicinity of the railway station. The temple was erected in 1950; inside, several fierce-looking statues of gods and warrior-like creatures watch over innumerable, gilded Buddha figures standing in rows of niches. Within the temple grounds there is also a ten-storeyed Indian pagoda.

A staircase leads one up to **Man Fat Temple,** dedicated to the monk Yuet Kai. He spent his time studying Buddhism and meditating upon the concept of immortality, until finally he died. In accordance with Chinese customs, his body was later exhumed so that his remains could be brought to their final resting place. But his body was fully intact and emitted a yellow light. Thereupon it was entirely coated with gold and placed in a glass case for all believers to see.

If one follows the road leading southwestwards to Lion Rock Tunnel, one will arrive at the walled village of **Tsang Tai Uk.** The village was constructed during the middle of the last century by the Tsang Clan from Guangdon Province. However, before the fortifications were completed, the

pirates overcame the inhabitants, sequestered the children and thus managed to ransom all of the clan's wealth. After this the clan disintegrated.

During weekends Shatin becomes a focal point for betters and fans of horses and racing: a new racecourse was built here for the sum of approximately 60 million US-Dollars. The race track has a seating capacity of 70,000. Traditionally, profits from the betting are turned over to hospitals and other institutions for public benefit. Thus, there are many dimensions to the fact that life in Hong Kong would be more difficult without horse races.

Shek O (E10), small fishing village with narrow, winding streets, is situated on the southeast coast of Hong Kong Island. A number of luxurious weekend villas stand nearby. Since many of the beaches here cannot be reached by means of public transportation, they are relatively quiet. Shek O's golf course lies between the village and beaches. From the small peninsula of Shek O Headland one has a beautiful view of the South China Sea and its many islands and islets.

Stanley (E10) is a small fishing port and market town on the southern coast of Hong Kong Island. Like Aberdeen, Stanley owes its name to a British colonial minister. Nevertheless, it was a lively marketplace long before the British arrived. Today it is inhabited by both rich and poor, Chinese and Europeans. Stanley Market is actually a huge flea market where articles of clothing, ceramics, rattan furniture, metal goods, vases and handicrafts are sold. Many of these goods bear famous brand names, but are still quite reasonably priced.

Public facilities on the beaches are good. Tin Hau Temple was built by the pirate Chang Po Chai around 1770. He also donated a bell and drum, which were consequently used to warn his ships of approaching danger. Stanley Peninsula played an important military role during the Japanese occupation. There are still off-limits military installations there today.

Stonecutters Island (D9). This presently uninhabited island has a moving history. Following the 1860 Treaty of Peking, it was taken over (along with Kowloon) by the British, who first used it as a penitentiary (as of 1863). This venture proved to be a failure, however. Funds were lacking for a sufficiently large and safe building and soon, wardens, police and Parliament in London were voicing their protest over inhuman conditions there. Furthermore, in 1864, more than 100 inmates managed to escape together. Not one of those who escaped was ever caught again.

Ever since 1890 the island has been reserved for military purposes. Today it functions as an ammunition depot.

Sung Dynasty Village (D9), situated in Kowloon, next to Lai Chi Kok Amusement Park, both of which can be reached with bus line 6 A from the Star Ferry quay. It is a village recreating faithfully the architecture and life styles of the Sung (Song) Dynasty (960–1279 A. D.).

The houses and cottages were built and furnished in the styles of the era. There is an apothecary's shop, a tea house and a sake bar with seductive dancers. The villagers also demonstrate various kinds of traditional Chinese handicrafts and arts, such as painting and calligraphy. A wax museum features noted personalities in Chinese history, including the great chairman, Mao Tse-tung.

Guided tours are offered on weekdays; such tours may also include a Chinese banquet. Cultural events are then put on, like an ancient Chinese wedding ceremony, kung fu exhibitions, a show with trained monkeys, dances and scenes from local operas. At weekends one can wander through the village on one's own.

Tai Po (B9), small market town frequented by the fishermen and farmers of the New Territories' eastern coast. Fish, vegetables, fruit and sweets are the main products being sold at numerous stalls. Tin Hau Temple on Ting Kok Road is nearly 300 years old. Due east of Tai Po lies the famous Tai Ping carpet factory, where one can observe Chinese carpet-weaving techniques even if one does not plan to redecorate one's living room.

Tours are possible Mondays through Fridays from 2 p.m. to 4.30 p.m. and can be arranged through the Hong Kong Tourist Association.

Tolo Harbour (B10). Twice daily, at 7.25 a.m. and 3.15 p.m., a boat departs from Tai Po Kau Ferry Pier on a tour of Tolo Harbour (Tai Po Hoi). It plies its way from village to village, island to island. Most of the stops are very brief. Some of the places on the way can only be reached with this particular ferry.

Tsimshatsui (D9), southernmost part of Kowloon Peninsula and the downtown area. Here one will find an admixture of modern and traditional shopping facilities, colonial and new hotels, fancy restaurants and cook-shops, flashy nightclubs and simple bars – in short, just about all the contrasts that Hong Kong has to offer.

Shopping centres like Ocean Centre, New World Centre and Star Ferry House are well worth visiting. They have a good selection of Chinese arts and crafts. Countless stores line Nathan Road. At night, Yaumatei district (particularly Temple Street) turns into a Poor Man's Nightclub with lots of stalls, cookshops and atmosphere.

Hong Kong's Space Museum is situated on the very tip of the peninsula. To the east, between Salisbury Road and Chatham Road South, is an even more modern quarter with glassfronted buildings functioning as hotels and department stores.

Victoria Park (D9), a green landscape right in the middle of the city, representing the borderline between Wanchai and Causeway Bay. Every morning, sometime between 5 a.m. and 7 a.m., a great number of Chinese gather here to practice taijiquan (tai chi chuan, usually translated erroneously as "shadow boxing"). It is the slower, "soft" form of exercises aimed at training movement, breathing and concentration, which in their faster or "hard" form are known as kung fu. The latter is also different in that it employs weapons such as canes, swords and lances.

During the rest of the day, the park is frequented by amahs (female Chinese baby-sitters or housemaids) and the children in their care, as well as by young couples. The park also offers a number of sports facilities.

Victoria Peak (D9). The highest point on the island of Hong Kong (554 metres/1,818 feet) is simply referred to by the inhabitants as "the Peak". Settlements were first constructed along its northern slopes in 1860; however, by order of the governor, these were to be strictly reserved for affluent Europeans. Needless to say, the governor himself also resided there. In those days, everything had to be carried up the hill by coolies, including the European inhabitants in their sedan chairs. Today there are streets with regular taxi and bus services which, together with the Peak Tram (built 1888), make these heights easily accessible.

From the scenic platform of the highest station, and along the prepared trails, one has a breathtaking, much-photographed view of the island's northern coast, its harbour, and, depending on weather conditions, over to Kowloon and all the way to the New Territories. One should also ascend to the summit again at night in order to enjoy the sight of the lighted city.

It is particularly recommendable to go for a walk around the Peak. A special trail with few gradients has been laid out for just that purpose. When the weather is clear, this trail also offers grand views of other parts of the island and the South China Sea.

Wanchai (D/E9) today has little to do with the world of Richard Mason's famous character, Suzie Wong. Shops, restaurants, sports arenas and art galleries have established themselves here now. In the Hong Kong Arts Centre, which opened in 1977, there are 15 storeys of lecture halls, studios, theatres, workshops and offices of numerous cultural institutes. International theatre groups, dancers and musicians give guest performances here.

Western District (D9), Chinese "old town" situated in the northwestern part of Hong Kong Island. A maze of narrow alleyways completely crammed with stands of all sorts – this is the way the less formal, but definitely more Chinese, part of Hong Kong presents itself. Every corner will have another surprise to offer. The shops sell meat, vegetables, household articles, tea, herbs, traditional remedies, mahjong games and whatever else is needed in daily life. Artisans – be they shoe or coffin makers – ply their trade in cramped, open workshops that partly extend out onto the streets. Of particular interest here are Ladder Street, Hollywood Road and "Cat Street" (officially called Lascer Street to wipe out the memory of the "cats" that used to

populate the bordellos along it). Today this area has specialized in the sale of antiques, some of which are actually supposed to be authentic.

Wong Tai Sin Temple (D10), Kowloon, is situated amidst housing estates, in the vicinity of the underground station bearing the same name. Wong Tai Sin is the "Fairy of the Red Pines"; she was especially revered by an immigrant family of the early part of this century (the members of this family erected the temple in her honour in 1921). Since 1956 it has been open to the public for a small fee or donation. The contemporary temple was constructed in 1973.

Numerous soothsayers, who tell the future with the aid of prayer sticks or by reading the palm of the hand, have settled down around the temple, an area which is much frequented by Chinese living in the vicinity.

Yaumatei (D9), typically Chinese district of Kowloon, with a large typhoon shelter for junks and sampans, and an atmosphere similar to that of Aberdeen. Each street has developed a certain specialty: Shanghai Street furnishes all kinds of bridal wear and trousseau articles; Canton Road has its jade market; and the flea market is on Temple Street. Four temples are located on Public Square Street. One hundred years ago, Tin Hau Temple was situated by the shore. Land reclamation projects have left it standing in the middle of the city.

(Jacobs/Krücker)

History of Macao

The name of Macao is derived from that of a popular Chinese goddess, A-Ma or Ling Ma, patroness of seafarers and fishermen.

According to legend, a junk sailing across the South China Sea long ago suddenly found itself in a raging storm. Passengers and crew had already abandoned all hope when an attractive young woman who had been the last to board the ship stood up and commanded the elements to calm down. Miraculously, the storm winds ceased as suddenly as they had come and the churning waters became smooth as glass. Without further incidents, the junk arrived safely at its destination, a tiny fishing village situated at the mouth of one of the Pearl River's tributaries, then known as Hoi Keang.

The young woman got off the boat without saying a word and, under the watchful eyes of her fellow travellers, walked to the crest of Barra Hill, from where she ascended to heaven in a glowing halo of light and fragrance. On the very spot she first set foot on land, a temple was erected in her honour. The temple, which can still be seen today, was named A-Ma and the small bay was then became A-Ma-Gao (Bay of A-Ma).

Centuries later, in 1513, when the Portuguese under Jorge Alvares landed at the estuary of the Pearl River, they asked the inhabitants the name of the area. The Chinese, however, thought they wanted to know the name of the bay in which they had dropped anchor and thus replied:

"A-Ma-Gao". The name was finally shortened by Europeans to Macau, or Macao, as it is still referred to in English today.

Thus also began the development of this tiny area into the (at times) most important base for trade with China. Failing to establish trading posts in northern China, the Portuguese ultimately retreated to Macao and settled there. For decades they tried in vain to secure their rights to this base in a treaty.

Such a guarantee was finally accorded them in 1557, after they had rendered the "Middle Kingdom" valuable service in its fight against pirates of the South China Sea.

Although China maintained its sovereignty over the area, the small peninsula quickly developed under the Portuguese into the distribution centre for all trade between China, Japan and Europe. The Portuguese thus maintained full control over this lucrative enterprise, which netted profits of up to 500 per cent. The Chinese also profited markedly from Macao's rise to riches. They charged annual interest rates and drew commissions on all trade. Paradoxically, Macao's success under the Portuguese was only possible with the total isolation of the Chinese empire from all other countries. It wasn't long before the Portuguese were the sole and uncontrolled agents between the two Far Eastern powers, China and Japan, and the European markets.

Porcelain, spices and silk were the main trade goods. The traders would buy them in China and then sell them in Japan for valuable silver coins, the only means of payment then accepted by the Chinese. Macao attained the status of a city in 1586.

As a result of the unification of the Portuguese and Spanish empires (1580), the Philippines and Mexico (with its vast silver reserves) had by that time already been incorporated into Far East trading relations.

Obviously the riches accumulated by Spain-Portugal in Macao did not escape the attention of competing colonial powers of the times. Again and again, British, Dutch and Asian pirates tried to capture ships laden down with silver bars, spices and silk on their way to Lisbon; often enough they were successful. The most serious attempt to break the Portuguese trading monopoly in the Far East came from the Dutch. In 1622 the Dutch East India Company dispatched a huge fleet from the area now known as Indonesia to capture Macao and oust the Portuguese from this part of the world altogether.

Even though most of the able-bodied men were away in Canton on business at the time of the attack, the plans of the Dutch did not materialize. A provisional army made up of Jesuit priests, Black slaves, domestics and a few remaining traders repulsed the attack, albeit with great losses.

After this event, the Portuguese finally fortified their trading base.

There followed a period of great setbacks for Macao: the closing of the Portuguese trading station in Nagasaki, Japan, and consequent loss of the trade monopoly there; splitting of the Spanish-Portuguese empire and consequent loss of trading posts in the Philippines and Mexico; opening of Whampoa (Canton's harbour) to international trade. With the establishment of British and French trading stations, Portugal also lost its monopoly on trade with China.

Macao's significance declined rapidly; soon it functioned primarily as a place of residence for traders from all over the world whose enterprises were situated in Whampoa.

Then, once the Chinese empire had finally allowed its subjects to live in Macao and, at the same time, the British had expanded their opium trade (and their smuggling activities), it not only became a refuge for politically-persecuted Chinese opposition leaders, but also the haunt of the Far Eastern underworld.

Nevertheless, the European powers still craved Portugal's possessions.

The British tried twice, in 1802 and 1805, to oust the Portuguese, only

Macao –
Geographically

This Portuguese overseas province is situated in the western part of the Pearl River Delta, directly alongside a small tributary of the great river and just 70 kilometres (43 miles) from Hong Kong. It is the oldest European settlement on Chinese territory, and it is tiny indeed. The peninsula covers an area of 5.4 square kilometres (2.1 square miles). The two offshore islands that also form part of the Portuguese territory, Taipa and Coloane, have a land area of 3.6 and 6.7 square kilometres (1.4 and 2.5 square miles) respectively.

Macao has 500,000 inhabitants; of these, a mere three per cent are Portuguese or of Portuguese descent. More than 97% of the population is Chinese. Ethnically, these belong to the Hakka and Cantonese, two farming groups, as well as to the Hoklo and Tanka, seafaring and fishing peoples. Both settled China's southern territory at the beginning of this millennium.

Despite the high proportion of Chinese inhabitants, Macao has preserved a great deal which reflects the European connection. Its unique atmosphere consists of an admixture of traditional Chinese culture and life styles and Portuguese mentality and architecture. People still live in junks and sampans; narrow and overcrowded street markets jostle between Baroque churches and houses that could just as well be many, many miles away, standing someplace in the Algarve or the old part of Lisbon.

Climate, flora and fauna are practically identical to those of Hong Kong.

giving up after China threatened to join Portugal in case of military conflict. The final military test of strength for the Portuguese in the Far East came in 1810, when they managed to defeat a fleet of junks under the command of the pirate Cheung Po Tsai in a great sea battle.

With the establishment of the Crown Colony of Hong Kong just 70 kilometres (43 miles) away on the northern edge of the Pearl River estuary, as well as the rapid replacement of sailing ships with steamships, Macao's decline continued.

Today, most tourists view Macao as a kind of side-attraction to Hong Kong, a place to relax and enjoy oneself.

Politics and Economy

Encouraged by the example set by the British, who declared Hong Kong a crown colony in 1841, the Portuguese finally dared to sever their territorial possession from the authority of the Chinese empire. Governor Ferreiro do Amaral declared the area an independent Portuguese colony and stopped all lease and duty payments to China.

This one-sided declaration of independence was not recognized by Peking until 25 years later. Macao's population remained fairly constant for over a century, until the advent of World War II brought about the immigration of a great number of Chinese refugees. Thanks to Portugal's politically neutral status, Macao was never invaded by the Japanese in the course of the war.

In 1951, the government in Lisbon terminated Macao's colonial status and made it an overseas province of Portugal. Nevertheless, because of the relatively open border to the People's Republic, China's influence – both politically and economically – continued to be greater here than it was in Hong Kong. This became very evident during the Cultural Revolution, when members of the Red Guard almost forced the governor to abdicate so that they could take control of the government; they were prevented from doing so at the last moment by the regime in Peking.

The fact that the Portuguese removed their troops from Macao in 1976 is a clear indication of the cordial relations between the administrations in Lisbon and Peking.

Ever since, Macao has officially been designated as "Chinese territory under Portuguese administration".

Portugal has granted it total autonomy in internal affairs. Head of government is the governor, who is assisted by an Advisory Council with 12 elected, and five appointed, members.

Macao's economy is based primarily on the entertainment industry, especially its casinos. Also of importance are textiles, clothing, electronics, chemicals and the toy industry. Traditionally, Macao is a centre for the manufacture of fireworks, crystal ware, porcelain and embroidery.

As in the case of Hong Kong, the economic and political future of Macao will depend upon the return of the colony to China. The treaty designating December 20, 1999, as the date of return has already been signed. It further states that China will assume control over its foreign and defence policies, but that the present economic system will be maintained for a period of 50 years.

Macao's status as a free port is also to remain unchanged for the time being.

Centre
of Christianity

The history of Christianization in the Far East is tightly interwoven with that of Macao, which has been the site of a Jesuit monastery since 1565. The first bishop of Macao was nominated in 1567. China and Japan also formed part of his diocese.

Particularly the Chinese, who placed a high value on education, equating knowledge with fortune and setting up wisdom as the highest ideal, had great regard for the philosophically and scientifically well-schooled Jesuit priests. One of the most interesting personalities to emerge among these clerics was Johann Adam Schall (1592–1666). He was summoned to the imperial court as an advisor and finally even raised to the status of a Mandarin. It was undoubtedly due to the Jesuits' political influence, which they gained in part because of their tolerance towards traditional Chinese religious rites, even pertaining to superstitions, that Macao managed to remain politically autonomous in spite of isolationist tendencies in the "Middle Kingdom".

Other than matters of faith, the priests also brought some very practical knowledge with them to the "Middle Kingdom". This included the introduction and diffusion of clocks and spyglasses, as well as sextants and other nautical instruments. At that time, however, the one Western technological achievement the Chinese coveted most was the cannon: with it they could put to practical use their own thousand-year-old invention, gunpowder. Thus it was the Jesuits who made Macao the centre for cannon production in the Far East. It was this particular branch of industry that ensured Macao's economic survival at that time.

As long as the Christian priests maintained a certain degree of parity in their missionary activites and "development aid", Christianity itself made good progress in China – quite in contrast to the situation in isolationist Japan. However, when the more pragmatic form of Jesuit missionizing was prohibited by papal decree in 1742 and replaced by an attempt to spread stricter doctrines, Christianity quickly lost whatever ground it had gained. As a consequence, the Chinese rulers forbade all further missionizing activities whithin their territory. The further spread of Christianity was thus stopped abruptly and pushed back to Macao. What has remained is the good reputation enjoyed by Macao's educational institutions; thanks to their traditionally high standards, they are respected throughout the Far East.

Macao –
First Impressions

It is a cool early morning in May and the air at the wharf where the ferries leave Hong Kong for Macao is fresh and clear. The contours of Kowloon, more than one kilometre away, seem close enough to touch.

At 6.30 a. m. the glass doors of the station open to admit passengers for the first tour of the day. Control of passports and other departure formalities proceed cordially; boarding passes are quickly distributed. Our seats in the first row guarantee us a panoramic view through the large windows of the hydrofoil. Slowly the craft backs out into the harbour and then sets a course for Macao. It traverses the natural harbour at reduced speed. A few junks and sampans come floating by as the skyscrapers and apartment complexes of Victoria slowly disappear from sight. A huge, laden container ship under Panamanian flag crosses our wake.

Soon we arrive at the outer perimeter of the harbour. The boat picks up speed and the hull comes clear of the water. Those on board would hardly notice the change in velocity if it weren't for the junks and fishing boats that appear to be approaching us at ever faster speeds before zooming away past the windows.

A breakfast snack is offered: sandwiches, fruit juice, coffee or tea – all at a reasonable price and quite welcome to most of the passengers at this early morning hour. To the port side, quite far away, we can make out Lamma Island. To the right of it are the barren, rocky islets of Sunshine Island and Hei Ling Chau.

Then, after less than 20 minutes, we are in the narrow sea channel between two of the most popular resort islands of the British crown colony: unsymmetric Cheung Chau on the port side and imposing Lantau on the starboard. Even though it is early in the morning, the first clouds have already formed over the ocean. Like opaque whisps of smoke, they cling to the summit of Sunset Peak, at 869 metres (2,850 feet) one of the highest elevations on Lantau.

Soon after we have brought the last of the islands belonging to Hong Kong behind us, we again sight land.

This time it is Coloane and Taipa, the two islands pertaining to Macao. Somewhat later we can make out the skyline of Macao: just a few, scattered high-risers and mostly southern European-style buildings. What a contrast to Hong Kong!

The hydrofoil takes less than 50 minutes to make the 70-kilometre (43-mile) crossing from the British crown colony to the estuary of the Pearl River. The huge sailing ships belonging to the taipans of the last century needed six to eight hours for the same journey; in adverse weather conditions it often took them twice as long.

The landing for the ferry is a wooden construction. Its bright paint has almost peeled off entirely, but people are already busy restoring it. In a matter of minutes our visa is stamped into our passports. A border official nods at us pleasantly: "Welcome to Macao – welcome to Portugal". And it really is true – in just 50 minutes the hydrofoil has brought us to another world. What impresses us most is not the modern construction of the jai alai stadium or the high hotel buildings along the waterfront, but the sight of a mini-Portugal in China.

The governor's palace, which is just being restored and repainted, could just as well be standing in the old quarters of Lisbon or Oporto; the villas dotting Penha Hill would most certainly not appear out of place in traditionally-oriented Portuguese cities like Albufeira, or even in Madeira.

And then there's the view from the summit of the hill: on one side a more or less modern port with its casinos, hotels and a few multi-storeyed apartment or office buildings; on the other, the crowded and lively Portuguese fishing village.

A modern bridge leads over to Taipa Island. One can make out the modern contour of a luxury hotel on the shore. On the other side, directly at our feet, the yellowish-brown waters of the Pearl River flow into the sea. A few junks and sampans are making their way along the river; because the border runs through the middle of the latter, such boats have to be registered in both Macao and the People's Republic.

We enjoy the quiet on Penha Hill, in the garden of the Residencia Episcopal, the (Roman Catholic) Bishop's Palace. Hardly a sound can be heard from the city below us. The singing of birds slowly erases the memory of Hong Kong's traffic and construction racket. Alicia, our guide from the "Direcção dos Serviços de Turismo" (Macao's tourism organization), urges us on. She still wants to show us the Temple of A-Ma, the Chinese protectress of fishermen and seamen of old Macao. Then we are scheduled to continue to San Ma Lo, or, as it is called in Portuguese, *Avenida de Almeida Ribeiro*.

Alicia belongs to the three per cent of the population that are of Portuguese descent – the remaining 97 per cent of the close to 500,000 inhabitants of Macao are Chinese. Alicia's family has been living in Macao for centuries. She lives with her parents, while her brothers and sisters have emigrated to Brazil. What are her feelings towards Hong Kong? The distance is just right – close enough to go shopping once a month and far enough to keep the hectic pace away from Macao....

Nevertheless, Macao has in fact lost much of its former serenity, as we were about to find out in the city centre. Traffic in the narrow streets and alleys has increased in leaps and bounds over the last decade, as it has all over the Far East, thus causing a veritable chaos during rush hour. In spite of this, when it came to choosing between tearing down historical buildings to broaden the streets, as was the case in Hong Kong, or preserving the quaint buildings of the old part of the city and partially reducing traffic there, the administration of this Portuguese colony fortunately opted for the latter.

A Stroll through the City

We are standing halfway down the main street, San Ma Lo. Before us is the Leal Senado, the Municipal Council, a prime example of Portuguese architecture from the 16th century. Its facade was restored in 1876. In the hall we are greeted by round-faced cherubs who smile down at us from ancient stone reliefs. We ascend a regal, sweeping staircase that leads us to the large, cool courtyard. It is shaded by palm trees, just like the patios of historical buildings in Portugal and southern Spain. Another stone bas-relief depicts the former Portuguese queen, Leonora, surrounded by the highest of clerical and secular dignitaries, and by heavenly messengers seen floating above her head. Also remarkable is the ornate wrought-iron gate at the entrance to the courtyard. The wainscotted Senate Chamber fills the viewer with a certain awe. Of a more wordly nature, but of no less historical import, is the public library situated on the first floor.

The well-kept building made of white stone that stands across from the Leal Senado is called the Santa Casa de Misericórdia. Built in 1570, it belongs to the oldest charitable organization in the Far East. Beside it stands the Post Office, which is also a historical building. Towering above the square, high up on a hill, are the ruins of the former citadel.

We continue on our way through narrow alleys flanked by apothecaries (both Western and traditional Chinese), stores selling refreshments and sweets, neswpaper stands, restaurants, and clothing stalls.

Along Rua da Felicidade, in the former nightclub sector, we come across stores selling dried, salted fish. Following Rua dos Mercadores we arrive at the heart of the old city, the "Tercena". There we find a quaint assortment of one-room factories, craftsmen's establishments and artists' studios. We watch as carpenters fashion carvings on camphorwood furniture or work on family altars. Then we see tinsmiths and blacksmiths forming bedposts or pots, bakers preparing noodles, women painting wooden shoes, girls casting tin soldiers, herbalists selling tea, and stores that produce and sell red or golden wrapping paper. Just a little farther on from here stands Macao's characteristic landmark: the tall facade of St. Paul's Cathedral. The rest of the building was destroyed by fire in 1835.

Shopping

While most technical appliances, textiles and jewellery are cheaper in Hong Kong, one can still find good offers in Macao as far as antiques and gold jewellery are concerned.

The supply in Chinese antiques is quite astonishing. Prospective buyers should, however, know just what they are doing if they are planning to buy expensive objects, as sometimes only the price of the "antique" is real! Handcrafted imitations are also sold here (they will be designated as such); these are very good value for the money they cost. The centre for antique dealers is around the Rua do Estalgens.

Gold jewellery is not only inexpensive here, but also has the reputation of being finely worked. Here, too, as in all countries of the Far East, one should demand a certificate guaranteeing purity of gold and weight (in carats) of gems.

Another tip: most Hong Kong Chinese not only come to Macao to gamble, but also to purchase spirits. Prices of the latter in Macao are an absolute bargain. Remember, how-

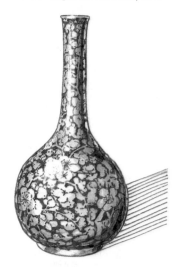

ever, that one may only import a quarter of a litre of wine from Macao to Hong Kong.

At the Casino

Hong Kong tries its luck in Macao. It is a perfectly normal Thursday as we enter the 24-hour casino of the Hotel Lisboa. A huge hall filled with thousands of people. In rows of three or more they stand around roulette tables, jostle for room at blackjack, storm the one-armed bandits with plastic bags full of coins, throw their Hong Kong Dollars on the gambling tables, cheer when their number comes up or stare stony-faced as their pile of chips begins to shrink and finally disappears altogether....

Now, at last, we understand why the Chinese are said to be "gambling-and betting-crazy". Housewives from

Hong Kong take their places at the tables. Office employees in smart business suits stand on one side, fishermen in traditional costume on the other. An entire family has set itself up beside them. Money is won and lost here round the clock. One floor above us is yet another gambling hall, almost as large as this one. Today the gambling industry provides the main source of income for Macao – in terms of taxes as well. Showing wise foresight, the government has forbidden its civil servants and employees to try their luck here, under the threat of immediate dismissal.

Other than the usual international games, traditional Chinese games such as *Fan Tan, Dai Siu and Keno* are popular. Their rules are not always easy to understand.

Besides the two gambling halls in the "Lisboa", one has the choice of the "Oriental", "Kam Pek" and "Jai Alai" casinos, and even a floating casino in the inner harbour.

Food and Drink

In Macao the visitor will find an ample choice of Chinese and Far Eastern cooking as well as international cuisine. The speciality here, however, is Portuguese food.

Bacalhau (cod) is the basis for most of the popular seafood dishes: you'll find it baked, grilled, boiled, stewed or marinated. Stews are especially popular here: the penchant for *feijoadas* was imported from the former colony of Brazil. The main ingredients are beans, pork, potatoes, cabbage and, above all, spicy Portuguese sausages. Sometimes sardines are also included. Hot spices also characterize *African* or *Goanese chicken,* which originated in Portuguese colonies in West Africa and India. Shrimps and crabs prepared with pepper and chilli are very popular.

The Portuguese love soups. Top of the list of favourites in Macao are *caldo verde* and *sopa á alentejana.* Both contain a rich portion of vegetables, meat and olive oil.

Among the rich variety of seafood available in Macao, there is one fish that has become particularly popular: Macao sole. Of course, there are also plenty of lobsters, oysters, shrimps and crabs to be had.

As for meat, every good Portuguese restaurant will invariably serve hare, breast of ox and oxtail soup as well as pigeon and duck.

Even the most exclusive restaurants are astonishingly inexpensive. For a three or four-course meal one pays little more than 90 patacas.

This price should normally even include a bottle of good Portuguese wine.

Hotels in Macao

Basically, what applies to hotels in Hong Kong is also valid for hotels in Macao. The standard is high, the service excellent. At the present time there are 14 hotels in Macao that can be recommended to tourists. The largest of these is the "Lisboa", with 750 rooms and two casinos. For a somewhat more unusual form of accommodation there's the "Pousada de São Tiago", which was built in the style of a Portuguese inn and harmoniously incorporated into the protective walls of the 16th-century Fortaleza de São Tiago. It is a highly luxurious and comfortable inn with 23 rooms, a pool and an excellent restaurant.

The Hyatt Regency Macau is considered to be the most modern hotel, with several restaurants, a discotheque, fitness centre, sauna, swimming pool, jogging track, conference rooms, ballroom and tennis courts. Other hotels: Estoril (89 rooms), Oriental (406 rooms), Matsuya (41 rooms), Metropole (110 rooms), Pousada de Coloane (22 rooms), Presidente (333 rooms), Royal (380 rooms), Sintra (236 rooms), Bela Vista (23 rooms), Central (160 rooms), Mondial (66 rooms).

Those who can should plan to visit Macao on a regular weekday. At weekends and on holidays it is absolutely essential that you make hotel reservations beforehand; for the Grand Prix of Macao (Formula III) rooms have to be reserved several months ahead of time.

Sports in Macao

Jai Alai: similar to the well-known game of pelota played in the Basque regions of Spain. It is the national sport of Macao. A modern stadium stands directly across from the ferry landing. Tournaments are held here every day, starting at 7.30 p.m. on weekdays and 2 p.m. on weekends.

Greyhound Racing: just about as popular among spectators as jai alai. The race track (Canidrome) is situated on the Avenida General Castelo Branco. Races take place Tuesdays, Thursdays, Saturdays and Sundays, beginning at 8 p.m.

Harness Racing: Macao has the first (opened in 1980) and to date the only trotting track in Asia. However, it has not drawn the number of spectators expected by the initiators and organizers of the sport. So far the ultramodern track with seating for a total of 15,000 spectators has had to be subsidized. The race track is located on the island of Taipa. Transportation by bus is available on the days when races are held.

Motor Racing: the Formula-III Grand Prix in Macao is one of Asia's motor-racing highlights. This race usually takes place on the 3rd weekend in November. Information and reservations are available through the Grand Prix Organizing Committee, Leal Senado, Macao.

Badminton and Tennis: limited facilities located on Avenida de la República. The tourist office can arrange the rental of courts in the clubs.

Watersports: a number of hotels have their own pools. Entrance fees for the public pool at the Estrada da Vitória are reasonable. The yellow-brown waters of the Pearl River estuary are not very enticing to swimmers. Still, the sea water surrounding the offshore island of Coloane is clear and the island has extensive beaches, e. g. Hac Sa Beach or Choc Van.

Bowling: there is a bowling centre with four bowling alleys on the ground floor of the Hotel Lisboa.

Squash: two courts are available at the Pleasure Long Restaurant, situated near the ferry landing.

Transport

Taxis: there are about 560 licensed taxis in Macao. All are fitted with meters and painted black with a cream-coloured top. Fares are reasonable.

Buses: public buses operate between 7 a.m. and 12 midnight. Lines 3 and 12 provide a regular service on the route between the ferry landing and the city centre. Regular bus services are also available to the offshore islands between 7 a.m. and 11 p.m. The bus station is located in front of the main entrance of the Hotel Lisboa. A ride on a bus can be a pleasant experience, especially during the summer when buses with open tops run.

Pedicabs: a slower but certainly more romantic alternative to taxis. The pedicab, or trishaw, is a tricycle carriage with seating for two passengers at the rear, powered by muscle alone. Like modern bicycles, pedicabs are fitted with a set of gears that allow them to operate on inclines. However, as some of the city's streets – especially in the centre – are quite steep, one cannot expect to take a pedicab everywhere. They are usually used for a pleasant ride along Praia Grande Bay. Be sure to agree on the fare beforehand.

Hire Cars: the only cars available for hire in Macao are the small, jeep-like "Mokes", which are painted in garish colours. In order to hire such a vehicle you must be 21 years of age and in possession of a valid international driving licence showing at least two years driving experience.

Macao from A – Z

The grid reference behind every place name or tourist attraction refers to its location on the general map on pp. 134–5 and on the foldout map at the back of the guide.

A-Ma Temple (B1/2) lies at the foot of two hills, Barra and Penha, at the estuary of the Pearl River. This famous temple is dedicated to the patron deity of fishermen and sea-men; it is from the goddess A-Ma that the name of Macao is (indirectly) derived.

Barrier Gate (Portas do Cerco) (A2) is the gateway to the People's Republic of China. One may look through it, but to cross it one needs a valid visa. Some of the lorries here will bear two numberplates, which means that they are registered both in the People's Republic and Macao.

Camões Garden and Grotto (B2) are located north of the Ruins of St. Paul, as is the museum of the same name. It was in this extensive park that the poet worked on his national epic, "Os Lusíadas". A bronze bust of the poet stands in the grotto.

Camões Museum (B2) was named after the Portuguese poet and soldier, Luis de Camões. The building was constructed during the 1670's and it originally served as seat of the mighty British East India Company. It contains an interesting collection of historical paintings, porcelain and samples of handicrafts.

Canidromo (A2), where the popular greyhound races take place, lies in the vicinity of the docks, in the northern part of the peninsula.

Choc Van (E3) is the best known beach on Coloane. Here the visitor will find a small, modern hotel, the Pousada de Coloane, in which to relax for a few days.

Coloane (E2–4), the southernmost of the two offshore islands, has the most popular beaches. Its extensive pine and eucalyptus forests served pirates as a hideaway well into the twentieth century. Various archaeo-logical finds indicate that the island was settled some 3,000 years ago.

Dom Pedro V Theatre (B2), was built in 1872 in the style of Portu-guese theatres of that century. It is situated on the Rua Central.

Floating Casino (B2) is perma-nently anchored in the Porto Interior, the Inner Harbour.

General Post Office (B2), a histori-cal building, lies in the old city centre. The best view of it is from the Leal Senado. It is a fine example of Portu-guese architecture.

Guia Fortress (B2), was erected during the 17th century on the highest point of Macao. It is located directly behind the ferry landing and can be clearly discerned by those coming in from Hong Kong. The lighthouse inside was the first to be built on the coast of China.

Historical Archives: A display of letters, books and manuscripts documenting the history of Macao and its relations with Europe, China, Japan and Southeast Asia over the centuries. The most valuable documents have been photographed on microfilm, including 7,500 pieces dating from 1587 to 1786. The archive is housed in an interesting colonial building, which has been restored in an exemplary manner.

Jai Alai Stadium (B3) is situated directly across from the ferry landing, on the Outer Harbour. Jai alai, a fast-moving ball game, is Macao's national sport.

Kun Iam Temple (B2), situated on the northernmost edge of the city of Macao, is 600 years old. Attractions: a gold-lacquered statuette of Marco Polo (who is honoured in China as one of the 18 sages), a stone table on which the first trading pact between China and the U.S. was signed in 1844, and the "lover's tree" (two trees that have grown together at the crest).

Lai Chi Wan (E2), a small town on the island of Coloane, known for the fact that fishing junks are still manufactured here in a traditional manner.

Leal Senado (B2), the Municipal Council, is one of the most interesting historical buildings in Macao. It dates back to 1784. It houses, among other things, the Public Library and the chamber in which the Municipal Council convenes. It is situated right at the centre of the old part of the city.

Lin Fong Temple (A2) is located in the northern sector of the city. Centuries ago it served as a traditional residence of Chinese Mandarins when they visited Macao as envoys of the empire.

Lou Lim Ieoc Garden reminds one of landscapes on Chinese paintings and drawings with its winding walks, tiny lakes, brooks and ornamental "mountains". It once belonged to a rich Chinese family. The members of the family turned both house and garden over to Macao's administration under the stipulation that it be opened to the general public.

Macao Trotting Club (D2), located on the island of Taipa, is the only trotting track in Asia.

Monte Fort (B2), located uptown from the centre, is actually called

Citadel of São Paulo do Monte. It is one of the oldest buildings in Macao, erected at the beginning of the 17th century. In 1622 it went down in history as those defending it managed to break the siege by the Dutch fleet with well-directed cannon fire. Jesuits used it for centuries as a seminary for missionaries who were then sent out to China and Japan. Today it houses a weather station.

Palacio de Governo (B2), situated on the Baia de Praia Grande, a large conspicuous, colonial-style building. Its distinct and simple facade and its pink coat of paint will immediately attract a visitor's attention.

Penha Hill(B2), a small elevation on the southern tip of Macao offering a grand view of the city, harbour, offshore islands and nearby China. The seat of the Roman Catholic bishop of Macao is also situated here. The church is only open to the public during the Corpus Christi procession.

Pousada de São Tiago (B2), a hotel built in the style of a Portuguese inn within the walls of the Fortaleza de São Tiago. This 23-room, modern hotel is an insider tip among veteran visitors of Macao. It lies on the southern tip of the Baia de Praia Grande.

Protestant Cemetery (B2) is situated at the foot of the Ruins of St. Paul (the cemetery is north of the cathedral facade). It is the final resting place for a number of noted personalities figuring in the history of the area. Among them: Dr. Robert Morrison, author of the first English-Chinese dictionary and translator of the Bible into Chinese; George Chinnery, an artist who lived and worked in Macao during the 18th century; and Captain Lord John Spencer Churchill, commander of the British warship "HMS Druid" and ancestor of Sir Winston Churchill.

St. Pauls Cathedral (B2), Macao's largest church, burned down in 1835.

Only the richly-adorned facade has remained. It was designed by an Italian artist of the 16th century and built by Japanese and Chinese Christians. It is now Macao's landmark.

A wide, stone stairway leads up to the church from the old part of town.

Sun Yat Sen Memorial House (B2), a personal museum, is dedicated to the founder of the first modern Chinese republic (1912), Dr. Sun Yat Sen. He practised medicine in Macao for a number of years.

Taipa (C/D2/3), this tiny island (3.6 square kilometres/1.4 square miles) is connected to Macao by a bridge. Here one will find a number of smaller beaches, the luxurious Hyatt Regency Hotel, the University of East Asia and an interesting Buddhist cemetery.

Getting to Macao

Many of those visiting Hong Kong also take the opportunity of embarking upon an excursion to Macao, the oldest European settlement in China. This small Portuguese colony lies just short of 65 km (40 miles) southwest of Hong Kong, on the other side of the Pearl River estuary.

It takes 55 minutes to get there by jetfoil, 60 minutes by hovercraft, 75 minutes by hydrofoil, an hour and a half by high-speed ferry and at least two and a half hours by conventional ferry. Schedules change two to three times a year, so be sure to ask for exact departure times when booking your passage ticket (booking ahead of time recommendable, especially at weekends). The faster crafts depart about every half hour; ferries cast off two to three times daily.

Hydrofoil

Hong Kong Macao Hydrofoil,
Company Ltd.,
33rd Floor, New World Tower,
16–18, Queen's Road, Central,
Hong Kong,
Tel. 5-218302
or:
Kowloon Ferry Terminal,
Sham Shui Po, Kowloon,
Tel. 3-602937

Fares: HK$ 46 one way on weekdays; HK$ 58 at weekends and on holidays. Children over the age of 12 months pay full fare.

Departures: every half hour, from 7 a.m. to 5 p.m. in winter and from 7.30 a.m. to 6 p.m. in summer, from the Macao Ferry Terminal on Hong Kong Island or Kowloon Ferry Terminal.

Jetfoil Services

Far East Hydrofoil Company,
Shun Tak Centre Terminal,
Connaught Road, Central,
Hong Kong,
Tel. 5-457021

Fares: HK$ 57–66 one way on weekdays; HK$ 63–72 at weekends and on holidays. Children over the age of 12 months pay full fare.
Departures: about every half hour between 7 a.m. and 5.15 p.m. from the Macao Ferry Terminal.
Night Service: between 6 p.m. and 1.30 a.m. jetfoils depart every half hour for an increased fare of HK Dollars 77–88.

Hovercraft

Sealink Ferries Ltd.,
Central Harbour Services Pier,
Pier Road, Central,
Hong Kong,
Tel. 5-423081

Fares: HK$ 45 on weekdays; HK$ 56 at weekends and on holidays. Children over the age of 12 months pay full fare.
Departures: nine departures daily (after 8.30 a.m.) from Kowloon Pier.

Ferries

Shun Tak Shipping Company,
Hong Kong Macao Ferry Terminal
Connaught Road, Central,
Hong Kong,
Tel. 5-8593333

Fares: children under 10 pay HK$ 8.
Adults pay between HK$ 30 and
HK$ 150 (latter for VIP cabin).
Departures: the whole day through.

High-Speed Ferries

Hong Kong High-Speed Ferries Ltd.,
Hong Kong Macao Ferry Terminal,
Connaught Road, Centre,
Hong Kong,
Tel. 5-8152299

Fares: HK$ 35, 45 or 55 one way,
depending upon class.
Departures: three times daily, from
8 a.m. to 11 p.m., from Hong Kong
pier.

A departure tax of HK$ 15 is exacted for every trip from Hong Kong to
Macao. The required visa, which will
be handed out upon arrival in Macao,
costs 52 patacas.

Further information is available at
the following address:
Macao Tourist Information Bureau,
Shop 305, Shun Tak Centre,
200, Connaught Road, Central,
Hong Kong,
Tel. 5–408180 or 5–408198.

(Krücker)

Hong Kong –
China Tour

The four-day tour takes one to the
province of Canton, which today is
officially called Guangzhou. A Chinese express train goes directly to
Canton, the major industrial city in
the region of the Pearl River estuary.
Canton is known for its export goods
fair which takes place each year.

Canton is mentioned as a trading
outpost of the Tang Dynasty in a
document dating back to 714 A.D.
Since then its importance in world
trade has increased steadily. It was
here that Dr. Sun Yat Sen, "father of
modern China", established an institution for the education of leaders of
the peasant revolt in 1924. Its first
rector was Mao Tse-tung. In the evenings one can visit Guangzhou Park,
the centre of cultural activities in the
city.

2nd Day: Flight to Guilin. Connoisseurs claim that it is the most beautiful and most romantic landscape in
all of China. Here one should definitely go to see the Reed Pipe Grotto
with its spectacular limestone caverns
as well as the city centre with its
"Lone Rock of Beauty".

3rd Day: A boat ride down the Li
River, past a mountainous landscape
with extensive bamboo forests, to
Yangshou, a village that may be visited. Overnight accommodation in
Guilin.

4th Day: In the morning one has
the chance to walk around the city of
Guilin. The flight back to Canton

departs in the afternoon; from Canton the journey continues to Hong Kong.

<u>Please note:</u> You will need a visa to enter the People's Republic of China. Travel agents generally apply in advance for visas for their clients (i. e., if you are travelling as part of a

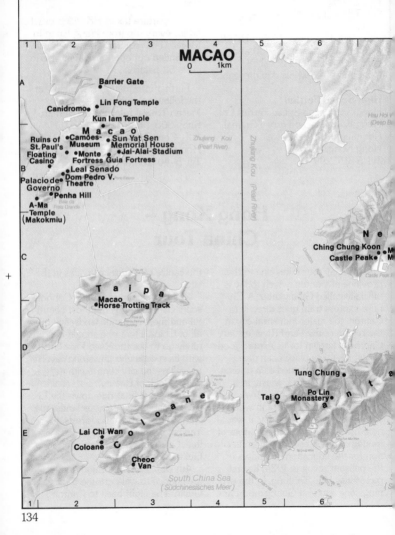

group, or if you have booked a package holiday, formalities will normally have been taken care of). Individual travellers should inquire about regulations before they leave for Hong Kong (any travel agent with Hong Kong on their programme should be able to help).

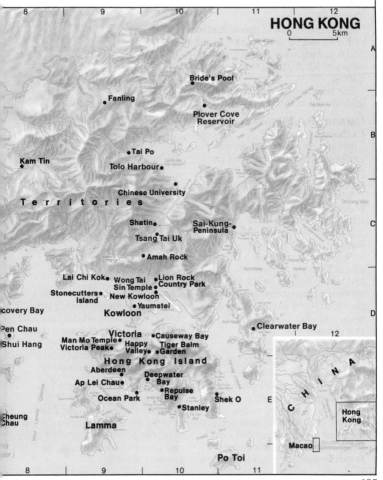

HONG KONG

Useful Information

Hong Kong

Currency
The national currency in Hong Kong is the Hong Kong dollar (HK$). 1 HK$ = 100 cents.

Coins are minted in denominations of 10, 20 and 50 cents as well as 1, 2 and 5 dollars; notes are printed in values of 10, 20, 50, 100 and 1,000 dollars.

For current exchange rates see foldout map at the back of the guide.

Currency Regulations and Exchange
There are no restrictions on the amount of foreign or national currency that may be imported or exported.

You are advised to bring traveller's cheques in U. S. dollars or pounds sterling. However, you will have little trouble converting free-circulating foreign currency in Hong Kong.

Major credit cards are accepted in almost all stores, restaurants, bars and hotels. Besides banks, there are numerous money changers throughout Hong Kong who generally offer better rates but also have higher service charges.

Entry Formalities
British citizens may stay in Hong Kong for a period of six months without a visa. Nationals of other Commonwealth countries do not require visas for a visit not exceeding three months; U. S. national need no visas for a visit not exceeding one month. Other nationals should inquire at a British embassy or consulate prior to departure (most visitors can enter Hong Kong without a visa for a stay of 7 days to 3 months).

Vaccinations
Currently no vaccinations are required unless you are arriving from an area infected with cholera. In this case, you must have a valid international certificate of vaccination (issued no more than six months prior to your arrival in Hong Kong). Check with your local department of health.

Medical Care
Medical care is excellent. Most hotels have contracts with physicians who were trained in the U. S. or Europe. Apothecaries offer all imaginable medicaments, mostly British and American. As the daily rates for private patients in hospitals are quite high, it is recommended that you take out a special medical insurance policy for the duration of your trip, preferably in conjunction with coverage in case of accident and theft.

Customs Regulations
Articles for personal use are duty free. The following articles may also be brought in free of duty: 200 cigarettes or 50 cigars or 250 g of tobacco; 1 litre of spirits; 60 ml of perfume or 250 ml of toilet water.

Airport Departure Tax
Passengers over 12 years of age: HK$ 120. Passengers aged 2 to 11: HK$ 60. As only HK$ are accepted in payment, be sure to retain the correct amount when changing back any unused currency.

Local Transport

Underground: one way fares on the MTR (Mass Transit Railway) range from HK$ 2 to HK$ 5, depending upon the distance of your destination. Special "Tourist Tickets" – reusable tickets for up to HK$ 15 – worth of travel on the entire system – are available at all stations. Lines run every 2 to 3 minutes from 6 a.m. until 1 a.m., between Hong Kong, Kowloon and the outer districts.

Buses: bus lines will take you to practically all of the interesting places in the city and New Territories. Fares range from HK$ 1 to HK$ 7, depending upon distance covered. As the drivers don't give change, be sure to have the exact sum ready. Buses run daily from 6 a.m. until midnight.

Taxis: they are red with a grey top and bear a lighted "taxi" sign. Basic fare is HK$ 5.50 for the first 2 kilometres; every additional .25 kilometres costs HK$ 0.70. If you have the driver wait it will cost HK$ 1 for every two minutes; HK$ 2 is charged for each piece of luggage; crossing the harbour via the tunnel will require another HK$ 20. The cabs are all fitted with meters. Complaints are taken very seriously here and the police has set up a special "hot line" for the purpose: Tel. 5-277177.

Minibuses: yellow and red vehicles with no set schedules or routes. Drivers usually only speak Cantonese. Just signal for them to stop; they will pick you up and drop you off wherever you want to go. Fares range from HK$ 2 to HK$ 6.

Airport Buses: a cheap means of transfer from the airport to your hotel and back again. Fares per person are HK$ 5 to hotels in Kowloon and HK$ 7 to hotels on Hong Kong Island.

Star Ferry: Hong Kong's traditional ferry plies between Hong Kong Island and Kowloon from 6.30 a.m. to 11.30 p.m. daily, leaving every 3 to 5 minutes. Fares: 2nd class HK$ 0.50; 1st class HK$ 0.70.

Wallah Wallah: these boats take over when the regular ferries stop services, plying between Kowloon and Hong Kong Island at night; they can also be chartered round the clock. Fares per boat and crossing HK$ 75.

Island Ferries: ply between Hong Kong Island and the outlying islands of Lamma, Peng Chau, Cheung Chau and Lantau on a daily basis. Fares range from HK$ 4 to HK$ 11.

Trams: run between Kennedy Town in the west and Shaukaiwan in the east, on Hong Kong Island. Fare one way is HK$ 0.60.

Peak Tram: the ride up 399 metres (1,309 ft) of the 554-metre (1,818 ft) Victoria Peak affords one of the best views of Hong Kong Island, the harbour and the countryside. It operates daily from 7 a.m. until midnight. Fares are HK$ 5 for adults and HK$ 2 for children under 12.

Rickshaws: a 5-minute ride will cost about HK$ 50 (ascertain fare beforehand). A pose for a photograph will cost between HK$ 10 and HK$ 20.

Car Rental: even though all of the major car rental firms have branches in Hong Kong, the often chaotic traffic situation makes renting a vehicle recommendable only for those who already know their way around. Prices vary according to size and make of car: from HK$ 120 to HK$ 300 per day or HK$ 700 to HK$ 1,800 per week.

Chaffeur-Driven Cars: minimum charge is HK$ 50 to HK$ 80 per hour for no less than 3 hours.

Helicopter: Heliservices (HK) charter flights for a maximum of 5 passengers. Information available under Tel. 5-202200

Opening Hours
Banks: from 10 a.m. to 3 p.m. Monday–Friday and 9.30 a.m. to noon on Saturdays.
Exchange Offices: 10 a.m.–8 p.m. weekdays, some also open on Sundays.
Shops: establishments in the popular shopping districts of Causeway Bay and Tsimshatsui are open daily from 10 a.m. to 9.30 p.m. With the exception of some large department stores, most shops are also open on Sundays. Stores in the Central District are open from 9 a.m. to 5 p.m. weekdays and 9 a.m. to 12.30 p.m. on Saturdays.
Administrative Offices: usually open from 9 a.m. to 5 p.m., with a break between 1 p.m. and 2 p.m. Saturdays only until 12.30 p.m.
Apothecaries: from 9 a.m. to 6 p.m., some until 8 p.m.

Accommodation
Overnight rates at first-class or luxury hotels vary from HK$ 400 to HK$ 1,200. There are, of course, more reasonable rates further down the quality scale.

The local YMCA or YWCA are recommendable. Their rooms start at HK$ 60 per night and correspond to good "middle-market" hotels. Beach hotels are available on the islands of Lantau (Silvermine Beach) and Cheung Chau (Warwick).

A detailed list of hotels in Hong Kong is available from the Hong Kong Tourist Association.

Tipping
Most hotels and restaurants add a 10% service charge to bills. It is customary for guests to add another 5–10% to the bill if they are satisfied with the service rendered. Taxi drivers expect between HK$ 0.50 and HK$ 1 for their services; the same applies to hotel pages and room service waiters. HK$ 1 per day would be a normal tip for chambermaids. The porters at the airport should get HK$ 1 per piece of luggage.

Clothing
Bring light cotton, silk or linen clothing for the summer; for the spring and autumn you should have a sweater or jacket with you. A light raincoat is recommended for the winter. Remember that more formal occasions in Hong Kong require the same apparel as they would in Europe. Some restaurants do request that their guests wear jacket and tie.

Laundry Services
Most hotels have a laundry service where you can have your clothes cleaned within a day.

Electricity

The voltage in Hong Kong is 200 V., 50 cycles. Most hotels will have adaptors available for guests.

Photographing

No problem in the urban areas and places frequented by tourists. The inhabitants of rural areas (New Territories and the islands) do expect the courtesy of being asked first if someone wishes to take their picture – a questioning glance or sign will usually suffice.

Language

English and Cantonese, a southern Chinese dialect, are the official languages in Hong Kong.

Diplomatic Representation

Consulate of the U.S.
26 Garden Road,
Central, Hong Kong
Tel. 5-239011

Canadian Commission
10th–14th Floor, Tower One, Exchange Square, 8 Connaught Place,
Central, Hong Kong
Tel. 5-8104321

Australian Commission
23rd–24th Floor, Harbour Centre, 25 Harbour Road,
Wan Chai, Hong Kong
Tel. 5-731881

Information

Hong Kong Tourist Association, HKTA Head Office
35th Floor, Connaught Centre, Connaught Road,
Central, Hong Kong
Tel. 5-244191

HKTA United Kingdom
4th Floor, 125 Pall Mall,
London SWlY 5EA
Tel. (01)930-4775

HKTA U.S.A.
Suite 200, 421 Powell St.,
San Francisco, CA 94102-1568
Tel. (415)781-4582

HKTA Australia
20th Floor,
National Australia Bank House,
255 George Street,
Sydney N.S.W. 2000
Tel. (02)251-2855

Recommended Literature

James Clavell, *Tai-Pan,*
London: Coronet, 1976.

James Clavell, *Noble House,*
London: Coronet, 1981.

John Gordon Davis,
The Years of the Hungry Tiger,
London: Corgi, 1974.

Robert S. Elegant, *Dynasty,*
N.Y.: McGraw-Hill, 1977.

John Le Carré, *An Honourable Schoolboy,*
N.Y.: Knopf, 1977.

Richard Mason, *The World of Suzie Wong,*
London: Collins, 1976 (original 1957).

Timothy Mo, *An Insular Possession,*
N.Y.: Random, 1987.

Han Shuyin, *A Many-Splendoured Thing,*
London: Jonathan Cape, 1952.

Macao

Currency

National currency of Macao is the pataca. One pataca is made up of 100 avos. This curreny is tied to the Hong Kong dollar.

Coins are minted in denominations of 10, 20, and 50 avos; notes come in denominations of 5, 10, 50, 100 and 500 patacas.

Currency Regulations and Exchange

There are no restrictions on the amount of currency which can be brought into or taken out of Macao. Foreign currency and traveller's cheques may be exchanged at hotels, banks and licensed money changers. International credit cards are accepted at many hotels and restaurants.

Entry Formalities

Nationals of Australia, Canada, New Zealand, the U.K. and the U.S. require only a valid passport for a stay of less than 90 days. Visas are available on arrival in Macao. N.B.: nationals of countries that do not maintain diplomatic relations with Portugal must obtain a visa from a Portuguese consulate overseas before they arrive in Macao.

Health

International vaccination certificates are not normally required unless tourists are arriving from an area infected with cholera. Enquire at your local health department.

Customs Regulations

Other than drugs and weapons, both of which are prohibited, there are no customs formalities affecting tourists. Remember, however, that if you travel from Macao to Hong Kong, the customs authorities of the latter allow only one bottle of wine and 200 cigarettes or 50 cigars or 250 g of tobacco to be taken into the British colony duty free.

Electricity

In the old part of Macao it is 110 V, 50 cycles; in the modern sectors it is 220 V, 50 cycles.

Clothing

Light cotton wear in summer; sweater and coat needed in winter. Casual wear is common, even in the casinos.

Information

Department of Tourism

Travessa do Paiva
Macao
Tel. 77218, 75156

Portuguese National Tourist Office

New Bond Street House
1/5 New Bond Street,
London WIY ONP
Tel. (01)493-3873

Macao Tourist Information Bureau

3133 Lake Hollywood Drive
P.O. Box 1860,
Los Angeles, CA 90078
Tel. (213)851-3402

Macao Tourist Information Board

475 Main Street
Vancouver, B.C.,
Canada V6A 2T7
Tel. (604)687-3316

Macao Tourist Information Bureau

Suite 604, 6th Floor,
135 Macquarie Street,
Sydney, NSW 2000
Tel. (02)241-3334

Please note:
Every effort was made to ensure that the information given was correct at the time of publication.

However, as it is not possible for any travel guide to keep abreast of all changes regarding passport formalities, rates of exchange, prices, etc., you are advised to contact the appropriate authorities (embassy, bank, tourist office…) when planning your holiday.

The publishers would be pleased to hear about any omissions or errors.

Index

Contents

Hildebrand's Travel Guides

Vol. 1 Sri Lanka (Ceylon)
Professor Manfred Domrös and
Rosemarie Noack

Vol. 3 India, Nepal
Klaus Wolff

Vol. 4 Thailand, Burma
Dr. Dieter Rumpf

Vol. 5 Malaysia, Singapore
Kurt Goetz Huehn

Vol. 6 Indonesia
Kurt Goetz Huehn

Vol. 8 Hong Kong
Dieter Jacobs and
Franz-Joseph Krücker

Vol. 9 Taiwan
Professor Peter Thiele

Vol. 10 Australia
Michael Schweizer and
Heinrich von Bristow

Vol. 11 Kenya
Reinhard Künkel and
Nana Claudia Nenzel
Contributions by
Dr. Arnd Wünschmann,
Dr. Angelika Tunis and
Wolfgang Freihen

Vol. 13 Jamaica
Tino Greif and Dieter Jacobs

**Vol. 14 Hispaniola (Haiti,
Dominican Republic)**
Tino Greif and Dr. Gerhard Beese
Contribution by Wolfgang Freihen

Vol. 15 Seychelles
Clausjürgen Eicke
Contributions by Christine Hede-
gaard and Wolfgang Debelius

Vol. 16 South Africa
Peter Gerisch and Clausjürgen Eicke
Contributions by Hella Tarara

Vol. 17 Mauritius
Clausjürgen Eicke
Contributions by Peter Gerisch,
Joachim Laux and Frank Siegfried

Vol. 18 China
Manfred Morgenstern

Vol. 19 Japan
Dr. Norbert Hormuth

Vol. 21 Mexico
Matthias von Debschitz and
Dr. Wolfgang Thieme
Contributions by Werner Schmidt,
Rudolf Wicker, Dr. Gerhard Beese,
Hans-Horst Skupy, Ortrun Egelkraut,
Dr. Elizabeth Siefer, Robert Valerio

Vol. 24 Korea
Dr. Dieter Rumpf and
Professor Peter Thiele

Vol. 25 New Zealand
Robert Sowman and
Johannes Schultz-Tesmar

Vol. 26 France
Uwe Anhäuser
Contribution by Wolfgang Freihen

Hildebrand's Travel Maps

1. Balearic Islands Majorca
   1:185,000, Minorca, Ibiza,
   Formentera 1:125,000

2. Tenerife 1:100,000,
   La Palma, Gomera,
   Hierro 1:190,000

3. Canary Islands
   Gran Canaria 1:100,000,
   Fuerteventura, Lanzarote
   1:190,000

4. Spanish Coast I
   Costa Brava, Costa
   Blanca 1:900,000,
   General Map 1:2,500,000

5. Spanish Coast II
   Costa del Sol, Costa
   de la Luz 1:900,000,
   General Map 1:2,500,000

6. Algarve 1:100,000, Costa
   do Estoril 1:400,000

7. Gulf of Naples
   1:200,000,
   Ischia 1:35,000,
   Capri 1:28,000

8. Sardinia 1:200,000

*9. Sicily 1:200,000
   Lipari (Aeolian) Islands
   1:30,000

11. Yugoslavian Coast I
    Istria – Dalmatia
    1:400,000
    General Map 1:2,000,000

12. Yugoslavian Coast II
    Southern Dalmatia –
    Montenegro 1:400,000
    General Map 1:2,000,000

13. Crete 1:200,000

15. Corsica 1:200,000

16. Cyprus 1:350,000

17. Israel 1:360,000

18. Egypt 1:1,500,000

19. Tunisia 1:900,000

20. Morocco 1:900,000

21. New Zealand
    1:2,000,000

22. Sri Lanka (Ceylon),
    Maldive Islands
    1:750,000

23. Jamaica 1:345,000
    Caribbean 1:4,840,000

24. United States,
    Southern Canada
    1:6,400,000

25. India 1:4,255,000

26. Thailand, Burma,
    Malaysia 1:2,800,000,
    Singapore 1:139,000

27. Western Indonesia
    1:12,700,000,
    Sumatra 1:3,570,000,
    Java 1:1,887,000,
    Bali 1:597,000,
    Celebes 1:3,226,000

28. Hong Kong 1:116,000,
    Macao 1:36,000

29. Taiwan 1:700,000

30. Philippines 1:2,860,000

31. Australia 1:5,315,000

32. South Africa 1:3,360,000

33. Seychelles General Map
    1:6,000,000,
    Mahé 1:96,000,
    Praslin 1:65,000,
    La Digue 1:52,000,
    Silhouette 1:84,000,
    Frégate 1:25,000

34. Hispaniola (Haiti,
    Dominican Republic)
    1:816,000

35. Soviet Union General
    Map 1:15,700,000,
    Western Soviet Union
    1:9,750,000,
    Black Sea Coast
    1:3,500,000

*37. Madeira

38. Mauritius 1:125,000

39. Malta 1:38,000

40. Majorca 1:125,000,
    Cabrera 1:75,000

41. Turkey 1:1,655,000

42. Cuba 1:1,100,000

43. Mexico 1:3,000,000

44. Korea 1:800,000

45. Japan 1:1,600,000

46. China 1:5,400,000

47. United States
    The West 1:3,500,000

48. United States
    The East 1:3,500,000

49. East Africa 1:2,700,000

50. Greece: Peloponnese,
    Southern Mainland,
    1:400,000

51. Europe 1:2,000,000
    Central Europe
    1:2,000,000
    Southern Europe
    1:2,000,000

52. Portugal 1:500,000

53. Puerto Rico,
    Virgin Islands, St. Croix
    1:294,000

54. The Caribbean
    Guadeloupe 1:165,000
    Martinique 1:125,000
    St. Lucia 1:180,000
    St. Martin 1:105,000
    Barthélemy 1:60,000
    Dominica 1:175,000
    General Map 1:5,000,000

55. Réunion 1:127,000

56. Czechoslovakia
    1:700,000

57. Hungary 1:600,000

59. United States, Southern
    Canada 1:3,500,000

    California 1:700,000

    The Southern Rockies &
    Grand Canyon Country
    1:700,000

*in preparation

Personal Notes

Personal Notes

Personal Notes

Personal Notes

Personal Notes

Personal Notes